WITHDRAWN

FACTS AT YOUR FINGERTIPS
EVOLUTION

BROWN
BEAR
BOOKS

Published by Brown Bear Books Limited

4877 N. Circulo Bujia
Tucson, AZ 85718
USA

and

First Floor
9-17 St. Albans Place
London N1 ONX
UK
www.brownreference.com

© 2010 The Brown Reference Group Ltd

Library of Congress Cataloging-in-Publication Data

Evolution / edited by Sarah Eason.
    p. cm. – (Facts at your fingertips)
  Includes index.
  ISBN 978-1-936333-01-1 (library binding)
  1. Evolution (Biology)–Juvenile literature. I. Eason, Sarah.
II. Title. III. Series.

  QH367.1.E95 2010
  576.8–dc22

                         2010015185

ISBN-13 978-1-936333-01-1

Editorial Director: Lindsey Lowe
Editor: Sarah Eason
Proofreader: Jolyon Goddard
Designer: Paul Myerscough
Design Manager: David Poole
Children's Publisher: Anne O'Daly
Production Director: Alastair Gourlay

Printed in the United States of America

Picture Credits

Abbreviations: b=bottom; c=center; t=top; l=left; r=right.

Front Cover: Shutterstock: CSP
Back Cover: Shutterstock: Mark Higgins

istockphoto: Fanelie Rosier 56t; **Shutterstock:** Galyna
Andrushko 3, Aquatic Creature 29, Yuri Arcurs 59, Ryan
Arnaudin 55, Wesley Aston 19, Calida 57, John Carnemolla
9, Clearviewstock 46, Ricardo Verde Costa 42, Christian
Darkin 41, Dhoxax 36, Ecliptic Blue 1, Eric Gevaert 5, Julien
Grondin 51, Tom Grundy 44, Geoff Hardy 6, Hiroshi
Ichikawa 43, Eric Isselée 16, Sebastian Kaulitzki 33, Kletr
12, Mark Kuipers 45, Hugh Lansdown 31, Paul Maguire 4,
Mariait 8, Monkey Business Images 34, Namatae 11, Aron
Ingi Ólason 38, Khoroshunova Olga 24, Ozja 17t, Regien
Paassen 39, Pborowka 50, Photobac 32, Thorsten Rust 10,
Howard Sandler 40, Hermínia Lúcia Lopes Serra 13,
Sevenke 14, Elena Sherengovskaya 48, Skylinephoto 18,
Spectral-Design 35, Kenneth Sponsler 30, Studiotouch 22,
Wellford Tiller 58, Tubuceo 54, Ronald van der Beek 56b,
Jason Vandehey 52, Vishnevskiy Vasily 15, Vladimir Yessikov
20, Konjushenko Vladimir 17b; **Wikimedia Commons:**
Public Library of Science/Marjorie McCarty 28.

Artwork © The Brown Reference Group Ltd

*The Brown Reference Group Ltd has made every effort to
trace copyright holders of the pictures used in this book.
Anyone having claims to ownership not identified above is
invited to contact The Brown Reference Group Ltd.*

CONTENTS

WHAT IS EVOLUTION?

Evolution is the process of change in groups of creatures over time.

Species (types) of living things change over long periods of time to adapt to their environment. Biologists call this process evolution. Although it is a pillar of biological thinking today, and widely accepted, the theory of evolution was shocking when it was first proposed since it challenged religious views of how life on Earth began.

In 1859, the publication of a book entitled *On the Origin of Species* by English naturalist Charles Darwin (1809-1882) changed biological thinking completely and had a profound influence in many other fields as well. Darwin suggested that a process called **natural selection** could explain the variety of life. In nature more individuals are born than survive to adulthood. Certain individuals survive because they have some advantage over the others. These individuals are more successful in breeding and passing on the advantage to their young. This process is the driving force behind evolution.

Evidence that Darwin was right is abundant. There are fossils that show the course of evolution over time in certain groups of organisms, such as horses. Evolution is also supported by studies of deoxyribonucleic acid (DNA) that shed light on the common ancestry of different organisms.

Spontaneous generation

Many people attempted to explain diversity in the natural world before Darwin. A widespread belief was the theory of **spontaneous generation**—that species arose from matter such as decaying organic material. The appearance of maggots and mice in conditions that seemed lifeless suggested that organisms could originate from nothing.

Lamarckism

At the beginning of the 19th century, French naturalist Jean Baptiste Lamarck (1744-1829) developed a theory that suggested that different species arose by changing from already existing ones. He thought that favorable features gained during a parent's lifetime would be passed on to offspring—an idea known as **Lamarckism**.

Lamarck suggested that changes in an organism's needs due to environmental changes could make body structures increase or decrease in size based on how much they were used. Lamarck's ideas were attacked during his lifetime and later proven to be false. Today, Lamarck is

Evolutionary biologists study fossil evidence, such as this ancient fish, to figure out how living organisms have evolved over millions of years.

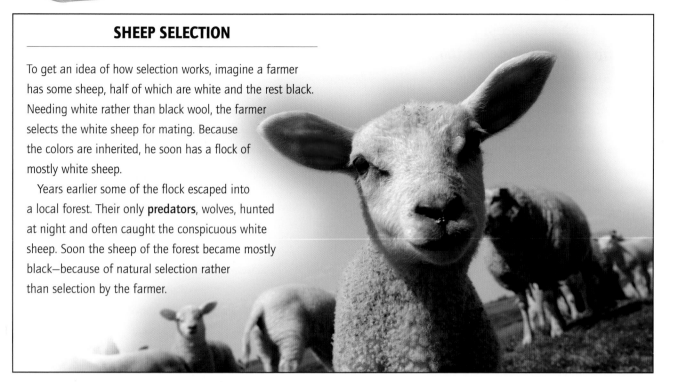

SHEEP SELECTION

To get an idea of how selection works, imagine a farmer has some sheep, half of which are white and the rest black. Needing white rather than black wool, the farmer selects the white sheep for mating. Because the colors are inherited, he soon has a flock of mostly white sheep.

Years earlier some of the flock escaped into a local forest. Their only **predators**, wolves, hunted at night and often caught the conspicuous white sheep. Soon the sheep of the forest became mostly black—because of natural selection rather than selection by the farmer.

remembered only for his discredited theory, and Lamarckism remains a byword for poor biology. However, modern biologists who criticize Lamarck have the benefit of hindsight. Lamarck was actually a very talented naturalist who made a number of important zoological discoveries.

Religion and evolution

Darwin's theories were at odds with the teachings of the Bible, which asserted that God created Earth and all the organisms on it. The argument continues to this day. People who believe that all life on Earth is the work of an all-powerful being rather than part of an evolutionary process are called creationists. They do not accept evolutionary theory as fact.

Studying evolution

Today, biologists study the process of evolution in a number of different ways. Population geneticists look at the different factors that affect inheritance. **Paleontologists** focus on **fossils** and other evidence to study how organisms evolved long ago in the past.

Ecologists examine how relationships between organisms and the environment they live in can affect the process of evolution. Studies like these provide crucial information for biologists. They interpret the evidence to figure out evolutionary relationships that may link different species.

SCIENCE WORDS

- **deoxyribonucleic acid (DNA)** Molecule that contains the genetic code for all cellular (nonvirus) organisms.
- **evolution** Process of change in groups of organisms over long periods of time.
- **Lamarckism** Outdated evolutionary theory that suggested that a parent's features changed according to use during its lifetime before being inherited by young.
- **spontaneous generation** Ancient belief that organisms could arise directly from nonliving matter.

EVIDENCE FOR EVOLUTION

Every feature of every organism on Earth provides evidence that evolution has taken place.

Charles Darwin's theory of evolution by natural selection is relatively simple, yet scientific evidence for it (especially in the light of recent genetic advances) is so powerful that biologists accept it almost universally. The world is full of evidence that supports evolutionary theory. This evidence ranges from the fossils of creatures that lived many millions of years ago to the rapid changes that are now taking place in bacteria that cause diseases.

The evidence of fossils

Fossils are the remains or traces of long-dead organisms preserved in rock. They have been collected and puzzled over for hundreds of years.

Before the 19th century, fossils were explained as leftovers from the biblical flood or as parts of creatures such as unicorns or giants. By the early 1800s biologists had begun to realize that many fossilized creatures no longer existed on Earth. They also noticed that some fossils were similar

This is a reconstruction of a Tyrannosaurus rex *skeleton. These fearsome predators roamed the land in the Cretaceous period, around 65 million years ago.*

EVIDENCE IN THE ROCKS

Sedimentary rocks such as limestone are formed by layers of sediment called strata. **Geologists** showed that younger strata always lay above older strata, except when they have been buckled and folded later. This discovery allowed biologists to follow changes in fossil groups over time. *Gryphaea* were a group of mollusks that lived on shallow seafloors between 190 and 75 million years ago. Early *Gryphaea* shells (1) were flat, but with an increase of silt in the water *Gryphaea* evolved to lift themselves off the bottom. Via several intermediate stages (2, 3) the flat *Gryphaea* evolved curled shells that are often called "Devil's toenails."

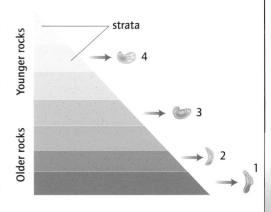

HOW DO FOSSILS FORM?

Fossils are the preserved remains or traces, such as footprints, of living organisms that died millions of years ago. Fossilization (fossil formation) occurs in a number of steps. Bones and other hard parts of a dead organism are gradually replaced by minerals.

1. A dinosaur dies on the shore of a large river.
2. The dinosaur is quickly covered by particles of mud and sand.
3. The sediment is slowly compressed (squeezed), forming rock. Minerals seep through the rocks and replace the dinosaur's bones and teeth.
4. Millions of years later paleontologists carefully pick away the rock to reveal the fossilized dinosaur.

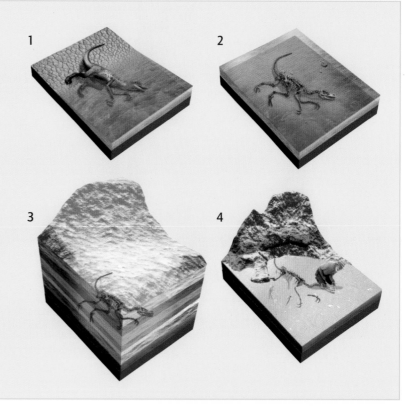

to, but not the same as, living creatures. This evidence suggested that they were distant ancestors of living animals. Geologists (people who study rocks) realized that the rocks in which fossils were found were sometimes millions of years old. These lines of evidence were in complete opposition to the teachings of the Bible, which held great sway over much of the scientific thinking at this time.

Paleontologists (scientists who study fossils) can follow how one form of organism evolved into another over millions of years. For example, around 55 million years ago *Hyracotherium,* the earliest known ancestor of the modern horse, lived in forests in North America. It was a small, dog-sized animal with five toes on each foot. Over many millions of years animals like *Hyracotherium* evolved to become larger and lost four of the five toes. That helped them run faster. Horse evolution did not move in a straight line but more by way

THE SPEED OF EVOLUTION

Scientists argue about the speed at which evolution takes place. Some scientists have looked at fossils and decided there is a regular rate of change, or evolution. Others believe a theory called "**punctuated equilibrium**" is correct. It suggests that there are long periods with no change, followed by shorter periods with very rapid change. The truth may lie somewhere between these two viewpoints.

of a "sprawling bush." Modern horses and their relatives form the last "branch" of this bush.

Signs in the rocks also tell scientists what the environment was like—for example, whether it was hot or cold, wet or dry. So, they can see from the fossils how living organisms have changed over time in response to major changes in the environment.

EVIDENCE FOR EVOLUTION

Modern-day horses have evolved over millions of years from small forest dwellers into large, fast-running animals adapted for life on grasslands.

RELIGIOUS BELIEFS

Before Darwin's work, biology in Christian countries was underpinned by a literal belief in the Bible. People thought that the Earth was created in seven days in 4004 B.C.E., and God also created animals and plants. Evolution did not take place because God had created perfect organisms. Fossils were explained away as creatures that failed to make it onto Noah's Ark and died in the flood.

Many Christians today, as well as people of other faiths, think Darwin was wrong and evolution does not exist, but instead, God created all creatures. This idea is called **creationism**, and it has some powerful advocates. Some schools, for example, are not allowed to teach evolutionary theory. However, creationism has been completely disproved by more than a century of experimental evidence.

Isolation and evolution

In different parts of the world there are animals that are similar to each other but are not identical. For example, jaguars live in South America, lions in Africa, and tigers in Asia. All are big cats, but each has a different coat and forms a separate species. Evolving from a common ancestor, each big cat adapted to its environment over millions of years.

A similar pattern is found in many other creatures. For example, there are similar large, flightless birds in different parts of the world, such as the rhea in South America, the ostrich in Africa, and the emu in Australia. However, some creatures that look similar do not share a common ancestor and have evolved from completely different organisms. This is called **convergent evolution**. For example, both whales and fish have streamlined bodies and powerful tails to drive them through water. Despite these similarities, whales are only very distantly related to fish. Each group has adapted in similar ways to the challenge of movement in water.

Moving continents

Scientists know that all the continents were once joined together but have moved apart over millions of years. That explains how groups of organisms have become isolated from each other, allowing them to evolve in different ways depending on their environment.

Evolution in isolation explains, for example, the geographical distribution of marsupial mammals. Marsupials include koalas, kangaroos, and wombats that carry their young in pouches. Marsupials once lived all over the world, but after the appearance of placental mammals (mammals whose young develop inside the mother) marsupials were replaced in the northern hemisphere. However, by this time the southern continents had already broken away from the rest. Marsupials were able to continue to evolve unchecked in South America, Australia, and Antarctica.

The ostrich is a large flightless bird that lives on the African savanna. Other birds in different parts of the world, such as the South American rhea, have also lost the ability to fly. This is called convergent evolution.

Antarctic marsupials disappeared when the continent froze as it moved closer to the South Pole. A few placental mammals, such as primates, did make it across to South America, but marsupials continued to prosper. However, most disappeared around 2 million years ago. South America and North America joined again, and placental mammals flooded south.

Just a few marsupials, such as the opposums, survived in the Americas. In Australia and New Guinea, though, marsupials flourished, free of competition from placental mammals until people arrived on the continent.

The evidence of anatomy

Anatomy is the study of the structure of organisms. Anatomists look at how an animal's bones, muscles, and organs are shaped and fit together. Biologists compare anatomies of different species to figure out how closely related they are. The more similar a pair of organisms is, the more likely it is that they shared a recent common ancestor from which both organisms have since evolved.

For example, all **vertebrates** (animals with backbones) share a common ancestor. The huge variety of vertebrates, including fish, amphibians, reptiles, mammals, and birds, suggests that the common ancestor must have lived a very long time ago, hundreds of millions of years in the past. By contrast, similarities between apes (gibbons, chimpanzees, orangutans, gorillas, and people) include an upright posture, large brain, and a flat face. They suggest a much more recent common ancestor. Biologists think that the common ancestor of apes lived around 15 million years ago.

False similarities, however, may occur as a result of convergent evolution. For a long time people assumed that vultures from the Old and New Worlds were separate branches of the same group, since they looked very much alike. Genetic research has shown this to be false. The vultures live very similar lifestyles, so similar features evolved in each group. Both soar high to spot food and use their powerful beaks to tear at carrion, while their heads and necks are bald to avoid feathers matted with blood. However, New World vultures such as condors are actually close relatives of storks.

Anatomical leftovers

Many animals have features that are of little use. These are called **vestigial structures**, and they are the remnants of features that were useful to the animal's ancestors long ago.

For example, whales have no hind legs, but they still have the remnants of pelvic bones. In land vertebrates the hind legs fit into these bones, which are at the bottom of the spine. The presence of tiny pelvic bones in whales proves that these creatures evolved from a mammal with four legs that lived and walked on land.

Snakes such as boas have a pair of tiny claws on their bodies. They are the remnants of hind legs. Unlike most vestigial structures, boa legs are still used, in mating. These claws show that snakes descended from four-legged ancestors. For a period in their evolutionary history snakes burrowed underground. During this time they had no need for legs, so as a result lost them as part of an evolutionary process. Later snakes returned to a hunting lifestyle above ground.

Marsupials, such as koalas, are found mainly in Australia and New Guinea, but they once occurred throughout the world.

FIGHTING BACTERIA

Bacteria are microscopic organisms. They cause many diseases, such as tuberculosis and cholera. In the middle of the 20th century, scientists began to develop a range of drugs that killed dangerous bacteria without killing the patient. The drugs are called **antibiotics**. Bacteria breed very quickly, producing many generations in a day. Natural selection swiftly reinforces any adaptation that helps bacteria cope with a new drug. Such a **mutation** spreads quickly through bacteria populations.

Drug-resistant strains of tuberculosis are now a serious threat in some cities. This is an example of evolution in action.

Another type of a vestigial structure is the tailbone in humans. You do not have a tail, but you do have the remnants of one—the one that your distant ancestors used to help them swing between tree branches. Mostly you do not notice this stump of a tail. However, if you fall and land right on the bottom of your backbone, you will bang it—and it will hurt. This bone is called the coccyx.

The evidence of genetics

Anatomical evidence for evolution is backed up by the science of genetics. By looking at DNA—the molecule that carries every individual's genetic blueprint—scientists can figure out how closely two different species are related and how long ago their common ancestor lived. The DNA of humans and chimpanzees, for example, is about 99.4 percent identical. Biologists suggest that their common ancestor lived around 5.5 million years ago.

By studying DNA evidence, scientists have found that chimpanzees are our closest living relatives.

SCIENCE WORDS

- **anatomy** Structural makeup of an organism.
- **antibiotic** Drug that kills bacteria.
- **creationism** Theory that organisms were created by God and do not evolve.
- **geologist** Scientist who studies rocks.
- **punctuated equilibrium** Theory that rapid bursts of evolutionary change are separated by much longer periods of little change.
- **vestigial structure** An organ or structure that has become redundant, or may be used for a completely different purpose than its original function.

Evolution is driven by natural selection. This process allows favorable adaptations that aid survival to spread through a population.

Within any population (regional group of the same species) of organisms some individuals are better suited to survive and breed than others. In turn, more young of the better-adapted organisms survive. This is called natural selection. It is one of the driving forces behind evolution, which is the process of change within groups of organisms over long periods of time.

Although a number of earlier thinkers had suggested that species may change over time, English naturalist Charles Darwin (1809–1882) was

Three of the original 14 subspecies (local forms) of the Galápagos giant tortoise have disappeared since Charles Darwin visited the islands, and only one individual remains of another subspecies.

the first biologist to figure out how evolution works. He looked at different groups such as barnacles and pigeons to show how natural selection takes place.

Discoveries on HMS *Beagle*

In 1831, Darwin set out on the British survey ship HMS *Beagle*. During his voyage Darwin made observations of animals and plants that made him doubt the accepted view of the natural world—that species did not change over time. While visiting the Galápagos Islands, 600 miles (1,000 km) off the coast of South America, Darwin looked closely at the kinds of giant tortoises that lived there. He found that each Galápagos island had its own **subspecies** with distinctive features. Darwin realized that the tortoises shared a recent common ancestor but had evolved in isolation on the different islands. He knew that the young of organisms that reproduce sexually (through fusion of sperm and egg), like tortoises and people, were not identical to their parents. Yet could these small variations lead to new? Was the Earth old enough to allow time for such changes to take place? While on the Galápagos Islands, Darwin also collected many finches. He found that similar but different species of finches had very

LAMARCK AND LONG NECKS

French naturalist Jean-Baptiste de Monet de Lamarck (1744–1829) was among the earliest evolutionary thinkers. He thought that use or disuse of a feature by an organism decided whether the feature was passed to young. Useful features would be handed on and others lost. A giraffe's long neck, for example, would develop from a lifetime of stretching for higher branches. However, Lamarck's ideas were disproved by later biologists.

NATURAL DIVISION

White-bark pines of the Sierra Nevada Mountains occur in two forms. At high levels, where conditions are harsh, they form low bushes. On the lower slopes, which are mild and sheltered, they grow into trees. At present the two types can interbreed, but the **hybrids** (young produced by the breeding of tree with shrub) are less able to survive than either trees or bushes. What might happen in the future?

Trees rarely grow very tall in colder climates since growing close to the ground helps keep them from freezing, and the roots cannot penetrate the frozen soil.

different beaks. Darwin wrote that "one might really fancy that . . . one species had been taken and modified for different ends." The finches helped Darwin develop his theory of natural selection. He realized that the finches had evolved to eat different foods, forming new species on the way.

Around the same time that Darwin was asking himself these questions, English geologist Charles Lyell (1797–1875) suggested that Earth was a lot older than people had previously thought—old enough, in fact, for extremely complex organisms to appear through the process of evolution. Armed with this crucial information, Darwin started to develop his theory of natural selection.

Forced to publish

Darwin spent around 20 years gathering evidence to support his ideas. Darwin was eventually forced to publish his results because another English naturalist, Alfred Russel Wallace (1823–1913), had independently arrived at the same conclusions. In 1859, Darwin's *On the Origin of Species* was finally published. Darwin suggested that since more individual organisms are produced than survive, there must be a constant struggle for existence.

Creatures that are better adapted to their environment are more likely to survive, so those that

MENDEL AND THE PEA PLANTS

Although biologists knew nothing of his work until after his death, Austrian monk Gregor Mendel (1822–1884) is today remembered as one of the most important and significant of 19th-century biologists.

Experimenting with pea plants, Mendel studied simple traits such as flower color. He found that parent peas pass hereditary factors (now called **genes**) to their young, with half provided by each parent. Mendel realized that he could predict the proportions of the traits in the young peas.

Mendel chose pea plants for his scientific studies because they have a short breeding period and distinctive characteristics.

possess characters giving them any advantage over others are more successful. These adaptations will increase in the population as parents produce offspring similar to themselves.

Darwin had a problem, however. He was unable to explain how features were inherited through the generations. He suggested they "blended," like mixtures of paint. Critics pointed out that if this were the case, good adaptations would be quickly diluted out. Darwin was eventually proven wrong on this point. The work of Gregor Mendel showed how inheritance took place. This showed how natural selection could occur, although Mendel's work was ignored by biologists until long after Darwin died.

After Darwin

It took many years of debate before biologists accepted that populations evolve over time through natural selection, and that species originate by splitting from other species. Evolutionary theory was based on fossils, on **biogeography** (where different creatures live in the world), and the development and structure of organisms. Over recent years these branches of evidence have been enhanced by molecular biology and genetic research.

Although he himself did not coin the phrase, "survival of the fittest" provides a neat summary of Darwin's ideas. **Fitness** refers to an organism's ability to adapt and survive in its environment. However, if the organism fails to produce offspring that also survive and breed, advantageous adaptations are not passed on. As a result, fitness is now measured in terms of the number of offspring that survive to adulthood produced by an individual organism.

Sources of variation

Inherited variations are now accepted as the raw material on which the process of natural selection acts. More importantly, biologists now understand how these variations occur in organisms and how they are inherited by their offspring.

MORE THAN ENOUGH OFFSPRING

A female mouse can breed twice each year and produces around six offspring each time. Imagine if all the offspring of this mouse and all subsequent generations survived and had young at a similar rate. Within just 10 years the descendants of the first mouse would number more than 60 billion! The world would soon be carpeted with mice. Why do you think that does not happen?

Mutations are tiny mistakes that occur when genetic information is being copied before offspring are produced. Mutations are the source of new variation.

Mice reproduce rapidly, producing many litters of pups during their lifetimes. Having such a high reproductive rate is vital because mice have short life spans thanks to heavy predation.

TRY THIS

Survival of the Fittest

This simple project shows the principles of natural selection at work. Make around 20 pea-sized balls of dough. Color half red and half green with confectionary dyes. Put all your dough balls on a green piece of paper, and put it onto a bird feeder.

Investigating birds will find and eat the red balls first. That is because the green balls are similar in color to the paper, while the red ones are more visible. In effect, the green balls are better adapted to survive and are less likely to be eaten Blending into the background like this is called camouflage.

red dough ball

green dough ball

robin

bird feeder

FORM AND FUNCTION

Sometimes organisms possess adaptations with an obvious function. For example, the limbs of whales and seals have evolved into flippers, which are much more efficient for moving through water than the land-adapted limbs of their ancestors. Can you think of any other adaptations these mammals have for living in water?

Mutations occur at random and are unrelated to the environment in which an organism lives, but they can be of major significance in evolutionary terms. An accumulation of mutations over long periods of time can lead to the formation of a new species.

Selection and color

Although they look different, black panthers actually belong to the same species as leopards or jaguars. To understand why, biologists need to study how genes are inherited. Cubs are only born black if they inherit a copy of the black coat gene from each parent. This is a rare event; but imagine if conditions changed, and having a black coat became an advantage. The number of black panthers would increase through natural selection. Over time leopards and jaguars with normal coats would become the rarer of the two forms.

Adaptation to niches

No organism can live everywhere on Earth. Each is adapted to its own **niche**, a specific place or role in an ecosystem, in different ways. An adaptation is a feature that helps an organism survive in its

A black panther is a leopard or a jaguar with a black coat. Animals that are much darker than other members of the same species are called melanistic.

By studying fossilized remains, scientists have figured out what saber-toothed cats looked like and how they behaved.

environment. Most adaptations have a genetic basis and can be inherited by future generations. However, many animals have behavioral adaptations, such as macaque monkeys that wash dirty rice before they eat it. These behaviors are learned and passed down through the generations, and are examples of nongenetic adaptations.

Understanding how adaptations work can be important when trying to figure out the ways that ancient life-forms looked and acted. For example, by looking at their bones, biologists have discovered how saber-toothed cats, a group that became **extinct** around 11,000 years ago, caught their prey. One group of saber-tooths, called scimitar cats, had long legs and short canine teeth. These cats were adapted for pursuit of small prey, such as antelope. The other group, called dirk-toothed cats, had much shorter, more powerful legs and extremely long canine teeth.

Dirk-toothed cats were perfectly adapted for ambush; they used their teeth to cause a massive, devastating injury either at the throat or in the belly of their prey. The fatally injured victim then quickly bled to death. In this way dirk-toothed cats could successfully hunt and kill very large animals.

 TRY THIS

Cat Adaptations
Look for adaptations for a predatory (hunting) lifestyle in your pet cat. You will see it has sharp teeth because it is a meat eater that must hunt and kill prey. It can retract its claws, allowing it to move quietly when stalking, but it can extend them to grab prey.

Physiological adaptations

Some adaptations, such as hibernation, involve internal metabolic (energy-supply) processes. Animals like bats hibernate to survive the winter, when temperatures drop and food is scarce. They build up reserves of fat in fall and then enter a state of torpor (inactivity) in winter.

During hibernation a bat's body temperature drops, its heart rate slows, and the need for energy

A male peacock's brightly colored feathers indicate to a female that he is able to father many healthy offspring.

AMAZING TAILS

A male peacock's tail does not help the bird survive. It is more of a hindrance that increases its chances of being caught by a predator. However, peacock tails evolved because the females favor males with the biggest, brightest tails. This is called **sexual selection**. Males with the best tails will produce the most young. Sexual selection drives the evolution of **sexual dimorphism** (differences between males and females).

The huge antlers of the male elk are a show of strength and help him attract females.

SELECTIVE DISASTER

Over thousands of generations male Irish elk evolved to have antlers of enormous size. This may have been due to sexual selection by female Irish elk. Females chose the males with the largest antlers to breed with, driving the evolution of ever-larger antlers.

However, this may also have led to the Irish elk's downfall. With a change in plant species over the elks' range at the end of the last ice age it became more and more difficult to find the nutrients needed to grow such massive antlers. By around 10,000 years ago the Irish elk was extinct.

falls dramatically. The bat wakes in spring, when it feeds as quickly as it can to replenish its fat reserves before breeding.

The cause of diversity

If a small population of creatures moves to a new area, adaptations to the new environment will arise through natural selection. In time the group may then differ sufficiently from the parent population to be classed as a new species. In this way natural selection is responsible for the tremendous diversity of life on Earth.

Updating Darwinism

During the 20th century biologists subtly revised Darwin's theory of natural selection. They refined it in light of advances in other biological fields. This update of Darwin's theory is called **neo-Darwinism**.

Neo-Darwinism accepts that evolution has occurred and is directed by natural selection, but the theory also incorporates evidence from genetic research, such as the importance of mutations. Neo-Darwinism also acknowledges the influence and affect that many factors other than just natural selection can have on evolution, such as **genetic drift**.

SCIENCE WORDS

- **biogeography** The study of where organisms live and how they got there.
- **fitness** The relative ability of an organism to survive and produce viable young.
- **genetic drift** The random loss of genetic diversity; especially important in small populations or ones on islands.
- **hybrid** Young produced by breeding between individuals of different species.
- **niche** The ecological role of an organism in an ecosystem.
- **sexual dimorphism** Anatomical differences between males and females of the same species.
- **subspecies** Subdivision of a species; a population that may have different colorings and a different range than other subspecies but can still interbreed with them.

GENETICS AND EVOLUTION

Since Darwin's time, biologists have looked at how genes influence variation and evolution in the natural world.

Although biologists have shown that evolution can occur through natural selection, it is not the only cause of change in groups of organisms over time. Evolution can also result from random changes in the genetic composition of a population, a process called genetic drift, while new genes may enter a population through migration from other areas. For evolution to take place, there must be a genetic basis to variations so changes that occur in one generation can be inherited by the next.

In Charles Darwin's time, the way in which features were inherited was not understood. Even Gregor Mendel, who had discovered and showed how characteristics were inherited, could refer only to "particles of inheritance." These "particles" were later understood to be genes. Genes form a code that drives the way all cells develop.

Genes are composed of deoxyribonucleic acid, or DNA. Genes are passed from parents to their children, who pass them on to their children. In this way, genes are inherited through the generations.

Long, coiled-up chains of DNA, called **chromosomes** contain sequences of genes. In animals and plants, chromosomes are found in the nuclei of almost every cell.

By the end of the 19th century people had observed **meiosis**, the process by which sex cells (eggs and sperm) that contain half the number of chromosomes of other cells are formed. However, it was not until the early 20th century that biologists realized that variation is controlled by genes.

Types of variations

Genes make us what we are. They control the way cells develop and function. Each of the genes inside the cells in your body is composed of a pair of **alleles**, with one allele provided by each parent.

There are two main types of alleles. Dominant alleles are always expressed regardless of what the other allele in a gene is. For example, the allele for brown eyes is dominant. People with blue eyes have a pair of alleles of a different type, called recessive alleles. Blue eyes occur only in the absence of any dominant brown-eye alleles.

MENDEL AND DARWIN

There is no evidence that Darwin ever saw Mendel's work. Darwin's idea of inheritance was based on a blending of characteristics, not "particles," as Mendel thought. This was a major flaw in Darwin's theory of natural selection, because blending would suggest that all variation disappears over time. Darwin could not explain this part of his theory because at that time nothing was known about DNA, or the genes that determine the way characteristics are passed on to future generations.

Eye color is controlled by your genes. If you have blue eyes, your genes include two copies of the recessive blue-eye allele.

TRY THIS

Learn About Variation

Take measurements of the height of children in your school (make sure they are of roughly the same age), and round up or down to the nearest inch. Then plot a graph with 2-inch (5-cm) groups along the bottom and the number of children for each group going upward. Your graph should look something like 1. There is a smooth change from short to tall pupils (2). This is called a continuous variation.

The shape of the graph (the red line) is called a normal distribution. Measure other features, such as weight or arm length, and draw another graph. Are these features normally distributed? Or is the graph skewed (slanted to one side)?

Variation is not always continuous. The ability to roll the tongue into a loop is discontinuous—you can either do it, or you can't (3). Another discontinuous feature is blood type, based on **proteins** on the surface of red blood cells. People can have either A, B, AB, or O blood type, but nothing else.

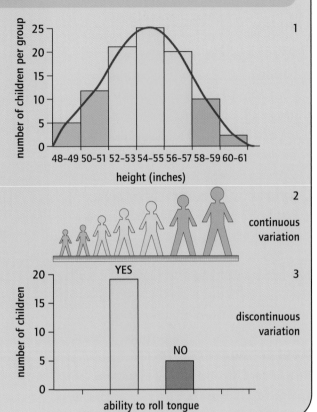

Some features, such as height, are known as polygenic traits. They are controlled by more than just one gene. Height, for example, is partly determined by specific height genes from parents; but other genes, such as those that control growth **hormones**, are also important. Height is also influenced by nongenetic factors, such as diet during childhood, and whether or not the mother smoked while she was pregnant.

What is the gene pool?

The variety of genes in a population (group of organisms) can differ greatly, although larger populations are usually more diverse. The total variation of genes is called the **gene pool**. A gene pool can shrink dramatically should a population become very small. It may lose further diversity through genetic

drift. Diversity can recover through migration, but new variation can only be created by mutations.

Mutations

A mutation is a sudden, permanent change in the genetic material of a cell. Many mutations are negative. They increase the chances of the individual dying before it can have young, and these negative mutations do not spread through the gene pool. Some mutations are positive. They help the individual survive and breed, and quickly spread through the gene pool.

Most mutations are termed neutral—they do not harm or help the individual in any way. However, imagine if conditions change, and the environment becomes much colder or hotter, or wetter or drier. These changes might make a neutral mutation

SEEING GENES

In 1910, U.S. scientist Thomas Morgan (1866-1945) used the fruit fly *Drosophila melanogaster* to study the structure of chromosomes. *Drosophila* flies are easy to breed in the laboratory. Their salivary glands contain just a few giant chromosomes. They can be observed easily because of their large size. Morgan discovered that banding patterns, which can be seen clearly on the chromosomes, correspond to individual clusters of genes. Why do you think this is important?

become either advantageous or disadvantageous. Those individuals that share this once-neutral mutation will prosper or suffer accordingly.

Fruit flies are perfect for genetic studies because they are easy to breed and have distinctive and easy-to-spot characteristics.

How do mutations form?

To understand how mutations arise, scientists had to unravel the mystery of DNA, the molecule that forms the genetic code. Success came in 1953 when English scientists James Watson and Francis Crick discovered that DNA has a double helix structure. It is a little like a spiral staircase, with each "step" made of one of four chemical compounds called bases. Each base always pairs with just one of the other three bases. When DNA replicates (copies itself) during cell division, mistakes can occur. They are mutations. Mutations occur at a faster rate when DNA is bombarded with ultraviolet radiation or comes into contact with certain types of chemicals.

Mutations help drive the process of evolution. They provide genetic variation on which natural selection—the process of survival of organisms best suited to their environment—act to create change.

DNA fingerprinting

Scientists study DNA to examine the relationships between different types of organisms using a

DNA PIONEERS

English scientists Francis Crick (1916-2004) and James Watson (born 1928) won a Nobel Prize for their research into the structure of DNA, but they were not alone in working on the problem. Fellow English researcher Rosalind Franklin (1920-1958) used X-rays to figure out the shape of molecules. Her work with DNA provided Crick and Watson with vital information about the molecule's structure. Franklin died without receiving the recognition she deserved, since her contribution to this major scientific discovery was, until recently, ignored.

technique called DNA fingerprinting. DNA is extracted from samples taken from the organisms and compared. Similarities between the DNA suggest a close evolutionary relationship between the organisms, while differences suggest a more distant relationship.

The degree of difference between the DNA samples also provides a good estimate of the time that has passed since the common ancestor of two different creatures was alive. When a species splits to form two new species, each new species builds up genetic differences through mutation. Scientists have a good idea of how often these changes occur. That allows them to figure out roughly how long has passed since the two species diverged.

Researchers are now using DNA fingerprinting to investigate the origins of life itself. They compare segments of DNA from very different organisms, such as humans and single-celled creatures like bacteria and protists.

SCIENCE WORDS

- **allele** Any of the alternative forms of a gene that may occur at a given point on a chromosome.
- **chromosome** Structure in the nucleus that contains DNA.
- **gene pool** The total variation of genes in a population.
- **hormone** Chemical messenger that regulates life processes inside an organism.
- **meiosis** Cell division that leads to the production of sex cells.

HOW DO MUTATIONS SPREAD?

Imagine a large population of butterflies (1). One of the butterflies has a neutral mutation (2) that is passed on, although it will not spread through the gene pool unless it becomes advantageous. Another has a negative mutation (3), which reduces its chances of survival. A third butterfly has a positive mutation (4) that increases its survival chances. This mutation spreads through the population (5).

1

2

Neutral mutation
Does not affect the butterfly but may be useful in the future. Mutation is passed on.

3

4

Positive mutation
Helps butterfly survive to reproduce. "Tails" trick a bird into attacking butterfly's hind end rather than its true head, increasing butterfly's chances of survival. Mutation is passed on.

Negative mutation
Loss of hind wing area means easier prey for a bird. Butterfly dies before mutation can be passed on.

5

MOLECULES OF LIFE

Every living thing is made up of tiny carbon-containing substances that include carbohydrates, lipids, proteins, and nucleic acids.

Everything on Earth, both living and nonliving, is made up of chemical elements (substances with one type of atom). The atoms of these elements combine to make molecules, and in turn the molecules combine to form matter—the solids, liquids, and gases that make up ourselves and the world around us. Some molecules consist of atoms of a single element.

Atoms are the components that make up every living thing, from a clownfish to the sea anemones among which it swims.

Other molecules, called compounds, contain atoms of two or more elements. The study of the chemistry of life is biochemistry, and the molecules of living things are called biochemical molecules. In living organisms the most important biochemical molecules are carbohydrates, lipids, proteins, and nucleic acids such as DNA. Biochemists who study biochemical molecules are called molecular biologists.

Essential elements

There are 92 naturally occurring elements on Earth. Living things are made up of fewer than 20 of these elements, although organisms use many more to keep their internal systems working. The most important elements are carbon, hydrogen, oxygen, and nitrogen. These four elements make up more than 95 percent of the weight of all the living organisms on Earth.

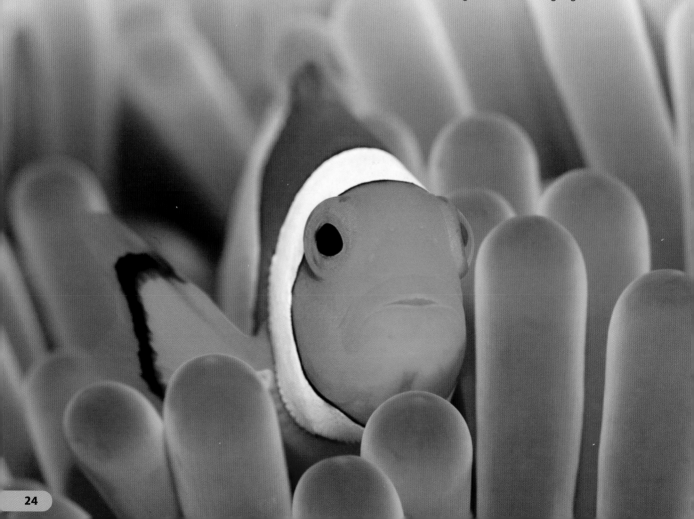

PERCENTAGE OF ELEMENTS IN THE HUMAN BODY

By weight the human body consists of around 61 percent oxygen, 23 percent carbon, and 10 percent hydrogen. Nitrogen makes up another 2.6 percent, calcium 1.4 percent, and phosphorus 1.1 percent. The remainder, less then 1 percent, consists of tiny amounts of more than 50 other elements, such as sulfur, sodium, chlorine, iron, copper, magnesium, and zinc.

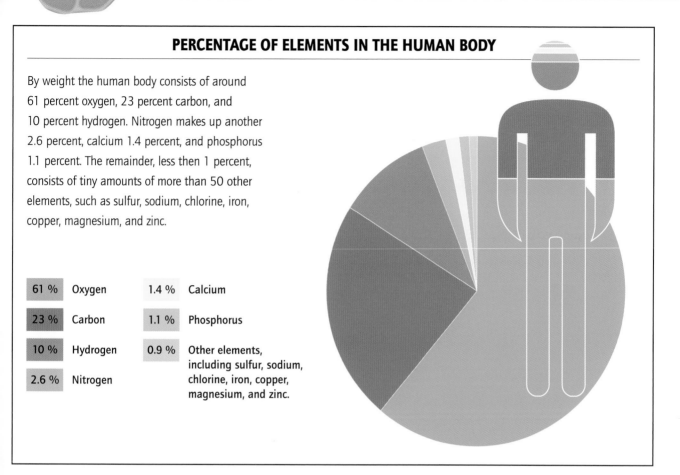

61 %	Oxygen	1.4 %	Calcium
23 %	Carbon	1.1 %	Phosphorus
10 %	Hydrogen	0.9 %	Other elements, including sulfur, sodium, chlorine, iron, copper, magnesium, and zinc.
2.6 %	Nitrogen		

Carbon chemistry

The key element in biochemical molecules is carbon. Atoms of carbon combine easily with one another and the atoms of other elements. They also link together to form long chains called **polymers**, with atoms of other elements attached. These chains can be straight, forked, or joined up as rings. They form the basis for the very large molecules that make up living things.

Carbon compounds are called organic compounds because in the 19th century most of the known carbon compounds came from living organisms. Scientists have now identified more than a million different carbon compounds. Some of them come from living organisms; but many others, such as industrial chemicals and plastics, are synthetically made (artificial). Compounds that do not contain carbon (for example, water) are called inorganic compounds.

WHAT IS GLUCOSE?

Glucose is a type of carbohydrate called a monosaccharide. There are six carbon atoms in each molecule. Five carbon atoms are joined in a ring, with hydrogen and oxygen atoms attached (see below). The chemical formula of glucose is $C_6H_{12}O_6$.

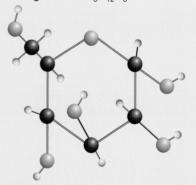

GLOBULAR OR FIBROUS?

The two main groups of proteins are fibrous proteins and globular proteins. Fibrous proteins are made up of twisted or coiled polypeptides. These proteins help make tough body tissues such as muscle cells and fingernails. Globular proteins are made of folded polypeptides and perform many tasks in the body (see below).

All proteins are made of chains of amino acids:

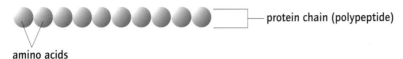

protein chain (polypeptide)

amino acids

Most proteins are either globular or fibrous:

Fibrous proteins are made up of twisted or coiled polypeptides.

polypeptides

collagen (a fibrous protein)

Globular proteins are made up of folded polypeptides.

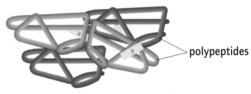

polypeptides

hemoglobin (a globular protein)

Examples of globular proteins

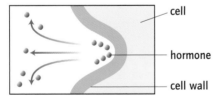

cell

hormone

cell wall

1. Hormones are released by cells to send messages.

sugar

carrier protein

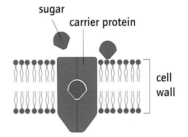

cell wall

2. Carrier proteins transport sugars and amino acids.

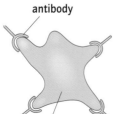

antibody

foreign body

3. Antibodies attack foreign proteins.

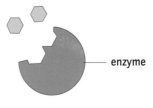

enzyme

4. **Enzymes** act as catalysts to speed up chemical reactions.

Carbohydrates

Carbohydrates are important biochemical molecules for humans because they provide almost all of the body's energy. The simplest carbohydrates are sugars called monosaccharides. A monosacchride molecule has a central ring made of atoms of carbon and oxygen. Carbon, hydrogen, and oxygen atoms are attached to the ring. A typical monosaccharide is glucose. It is used as fuel by animal and plant cells; it is burned to produce energy.

Monosaccharide molecules can join together in twos (making sugars called disaccharides) and in long chains to form polysaccharides. Glycogen and starch are polysaccharides. Glycogen molecules are long glucose chains with many side branches. Animals store glycogen in their livers and convert it into glucose for energy. Blood carries the glucose to muscles and organs. Starch is similar to glycogen, but its molecules have fewer branches. Plants store starch and change it into glucose to provide energy.

Lipids

Oils, fats, and waxes are all lipids. Fats store energy and protect organs with padding, while oils and waxes protect the skin and hair. Most lipids are made of glycerol or glycerine and fatty acids. Glycerol is a natural alcohol made up of carbon, hydrogen, and oxygen. A fatty acid is a chain of carbon atoms with hydrogen atoms attached to them.

The most common fats we have are lipids called triglycerides. A triglyceride is one molecule of glycerol attached to three molecules of fatty acids. The body stores triglycerides in fat cells. Turning glycerol into glucose produces energy.

Proteins

Proteins are the basic structural materials of all plant and animal cells. They control and carry out the chemical processes that enable cells to function. Proteins are called the building blocks of life because they are so important. Protein molecules contain

TRY THIS

Making Protein Glue
Milk contains a protein called casein. You can separate the casein from milk and make it into glue.

1. Put half a cup of milk into a small bowl, and stir in 2 tablespoons of vinegar. Keep stirring the mixture until no more lumps form.
2. Line a kitchen strainer with a paper towel. Hold the strainer over a bowl, and pour the mixture into it. The paper towel will catch the lumps in the mixture. Gently blot the lumps with more paper towels to squeeze out all the liquid.
3. Rinse out the first bowl, and then scrape the lumps into it. Stir in 2 tablespoons of water and half a teaspoon of baking soda. Keep stirring and adding small amounts of baking soda until no more bubbles appear. You have made casein glue.

In this experiment you will make a protein called casein by adding vinegar (an acid) to a bowl of cow's milk.

carbon, hydrogen, oxygen, and nitrogen. Many proteins also contain sulfur, iron, and phosphorus.

The cells of all living organisms make proteins from amino acids. Amino acids are based on carbon, hydrogen, nitrogen, and oxygen. Twenty different types of amino acids occur in living creatures. Cells join them into long chains of amino acid molecules to form substances called polypeptides. Then the cells shape the polypeptides into protein molecules.

Francis Crick (right) and James Watson (center, background) won the 1962 Nobel Prize for Physiology or Medicine for figuring out the double-helix structure of the DNA molecule.

Nucleic acids

Nucleic acids are complex molecules that store genetic (inherited) information within cells. This information controls the growth, function, and reproduction of cells and of the whole organism. The two types of nucleic acids are deoxyribonucleic acid (DNA) and **ribonucleic acid (RNA)**.

Scientists discovered the structure of DNA in the 1950s after X-ray diffraction was first used to look at the atomic structure of crystals. This led to the science of molecular biology. The pattern produced by X-rays passing through crystals revealed the positions of the atoms inside the crystals. Both DNA and RNA are long chains of molecular units called nucleotides. Each nucleotide consists of a sugar; a

HOW LONG IS DNA?

The DNA of a single *Escherichia coli* bacterium is about 4 million base pairs long. Stretched out flat, this DNA measures around 0.05 inches (1.4 mm) long—much longer than the bacterium itself. The DNA forms a ring that is squashed up small to fit inside the bacterial cell. This arrangement doesn't work for creatures with longer DNA molecules, such as humans, though. DNA in these organisms is wound tightly with proteins to form a material called chromatin. Human DNA contains around 3 billion bases. Using the figures for *E. coli* DNA, can you estimate how long DNA from a single human cell would be if it were laid out flat?

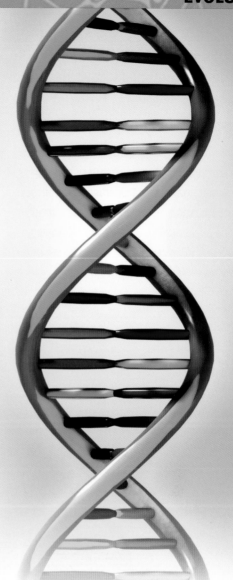

This computer artwork shows how the bases (colored rods) of a DNA molecule pair up to form a distinctive double-helix shape.

ring of carbon, nitrogen, and hydrogen atoms called a base; and a phosphate. A phosphate is a combination of phosphorus and oxygen atoms.

In DNA, the sugar in the nucleotides is called deoxyribose. The DNA molecule has two chains of nucleotides coiled around each other in a double helix. The bases of one chain are joined to the bases of the other.

Ribose is the sugar in RNA nucleotides, and a molecule of RNA forms a single long chain.

There are four types of bases in DNA, and each base contains a different combination of carbon, nitrogen, and hydrogen atoms. These bases are called adenine (A), guanine (G), cytosine (C), and thymine (T).

In RNA the bases are adenine (A), guanine (G), cytosine (C), and uracil (U).

DNA and RNA bases function in groups of three, called triplets. A string of triplets (such as AAA GAG ACA CCT) is said to "code" for a particular protein. In this way the triplet code dictates which proteins are produced in cells.

SCIENCE WORDS

- **enzyme** Protein that speeds up chemical reactions inside an organism.
- **lipid** One of a group of molecules that form oils, fats, and waxes.
- **polymer** A long chain of molecules.
- **ribonucleic acid (RNA)** Chemical similar to DNA involved in protein production.

GENOMES

A genome is an organism's complete set of genes. Biologists have decoded the genomes of several types of organisms, including humans.

With the exception of some viruses, the inherited material of all organisms is composed of molecules of deoxyribonucleic acid, or DNA. The amount of DNA in the nucleus varies enormously between species. As you might expect, multicellular creatures like animals and plants generally have more DNA than single-celled organisms. However, some single-

---

WHAT ARE GENES?

Genes are a type of code found inside cells. Formed by a chemical called DNA, genes are inherited by offspring from their parents. The code drives the way cells develop and function.

---

celled creatures, such as amebas, have truly massive genomes. That is because these creatures are **polyploids**. At some stage in their evolutionary history they have incorporated the genome of another species into their own.

Research on genome size has revealed some intriguing relationships. For example, genome size corresponds to the size of red blood cells in mammals, despite the fact that mammals' red blood cells contain no DNA. Lungfish and lilies have the largest genomes, at almost 40 times larger than that of a human. Land snail genomes are larger than those of water snails, while flightless birds such as ostriches have larger genomes than their flying relatives.

Exploring genomes

Since the 1980s biologists have begun to decode the entire genomes of a number of different organisms. Such genome projects are having major effects in medicine, in the treatment of genetic disorders such as cystic fibrosis, for example.

Even the genomes of identical twins are not completely the same. Environmental factors also play a part in shaping the genome of an individual.

THE MINIMUM GENOME

This experiment shows how researchers discovered that life's minimum genome contains just 337 genes. By mutating (changing) each gene in turn, the scientists could figure out which were essential for cellular life.

1. *Mycoplasma genitalium* bacteria have only 470 genes. Two are shown here, R and S.

2. A chunk of DNA called a transposon is added. The transposon enters the gene, mutating (changing) it so the gene cannot function.

3. The mutated bacteria are cultured in a nutrient-rich liquid.

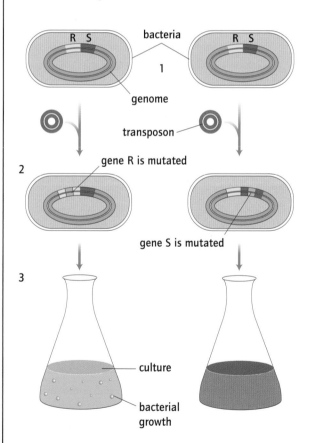

The bacteria continue to grow despite the mutation. Gene R is therefore not essential for life.

The bacteria do not grow. Gene S is essential for the bacteria and forms part of life's minimum genome.

The lungfish has one of the largest genomes of any living organism, including human beings.

DNA HYBRIDIZATION

Similarities between the genomes of different species indicate how closely they are related. To find out how similar two species are, scientists use a technique called DNA hybridization. DNA is isolated from cells of the two organisms and treated with chemicals to separate the strands. The DNA is then mixed together. A strand from one sample tries to re-form into a complete DNA molecule with a strand from the other sample. The greater the similarities of the base sequences of the two species, the more successful the pairing up is. DNA strands from closely related species form more new molecules than strands from more distantly related creatures.

Early successes involved the decoding of the genomes of fruit flies and roundworms. Later, the human genome was successfully decoded. Other genomes decoded in recent years include animals such as dogs, cows, and mice.

DECIPHERING DOG DNA

Since the completion of the Human Genome Project (HGP) biologists have begun to unravel the genomes of other mammal species. In 2003 researchers revealed a series of preliminary findings from a study of the dog genome. Using the DNA of a poodle, the researchers found that people and dogs share more than 75 percent of their genes. Many of the remaining dog genes code for features that aid a dog's remarkable powers of smell.

The research also helped the biologists learn more about the 400 known genetic diseases that affect dogs. Many of these disorders have human equivalents. Narcolepsy, for example, is a disorder that causes uncontrollable bursts of sleep in people—and in dogs, too.

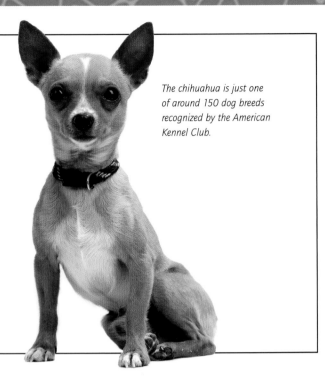

The chihuahua is just one of around 150 dog breeds recognized by the American Kennel Club.

Bacterial genomes

As you might expect, the genomes of tiny bacteria are very much smaller than those of multicellular organisms such as animals, plants, and fungi. For example, the genome of humans contains about 23,000 genes. A group of bacteria called mycoplasmas have the smallest of all known genomes. Their genome contains just 470 genes. With so few genes the mycoplasma genome must approach the bare minimum required for cellular (nonvirus) life to exist.

Using mycoplasmas, biologists have learned more about this lower limit in genome size. They have found that there are 337 genes that are essential for life. These genes are universal and occur in all cellular organisms. This discovery may lead to the creation of synthetic life-forms. Scientists could take the key genes and add genes for features such as tolerance of radioactivity. Such bacteria could then be used to clean up spills of nuclear waste.

Synthetic bacteria may be made soon. By 2003 synthetic viruses had already been created. Starting from scratch, scientists used DNA to make an synthetic version of an existing type of virus.

Genes outside the nucleus

In the early 20th century scientists found that some animal and plant genes did not follow Mendel's laws of inheritance. They then found that these genes were not located on chromosomes and were not even in the nucleus. They were present in organelles called mitochondria that provide energy for the cell.

GENE PROBES

Scientists can discover the location of a gene in a DNA sample by using a gene probe. A gene probe is a short length of DNA that contains radioactive elements. It releases radioactivity so researchers can pinpoint its location. The gene probe has a series of bases that bond with those of the target gene. To use a gene probe, the strands of the sample DNA molecules are separated. The gene probe is added to the sample. Because their bases are complementary, the radioactive DNA attaches to the target gene. The gene can then be located by detecting the radioactivity.

SWITCHING ON BACTERIAL GENES

Genes are usually switched on and off by other genes. However, other things can sometimes trigger a gene into action. When some bacteria are exposed to a type of sugar, a gene is switched on that allows them to use the food source. This gene is usually kept switched off by the presence of a chemical. The sugar binds to the chemical, stopping it from blocking the gene. That switches the gene on.

Mitochondrial DNA (or mDNA) is passed to young through just the female line. That is because the egg contributes all the mitochondria to the newly fertilized cell. The sperm has just enough mitochondria to get it to the egg but no more, and they are destroyed right after **fertilization**. mDNA mutates much more quickly than nuclear DNA does—mitochondria lack the suite of enzymes that iron out mistakes in the nucleus.

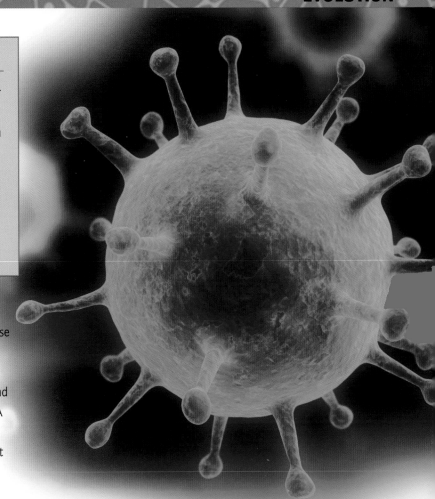

Viruses are tiny organisms made up of one or two strands of DNA or RNA enclosed within a protein coat.

Applications of mDNA

mDNA is used to trace family lines through the mother's side, and it has helped answer many fascinating questions about human history. For example, research using mDNA has proved that most Native Americans are descended from just six Asian women. The descendants of the women migrated from northern Asia to North America around 20,000 years ago. Native Americans then descended from these people. Similarly, mDNA research has shown that all people of European descent are related to one of seven women from various parts of Europe. The women lived between 10,000 and 45,000 years ago. mDNA has also been used to determine the burial place of the Russian royal family executed in 1918. Research has proved that human remains found in the Ural Mountains in 1991 are those of the Russian royal family.

Mapping genomes

Biologists began to decode entire genomes in the 1980s, starting with tiny organisms, such as bacteria, and moving onto larger ones, such as fruit flies. The greatest achievement to date was the completion of the Human Genome Project (HGP) in 2003.

SCIENCE WORDS

- **fertilization** The fusion of a sperm with an egg.
- **polyploid** Organism with extra sets of chromosomes.

POPULATION GENETICS

Population genetics looks at the effects of genes on the features of groups of organisms, and how and why their genetic makeup changes over time.

Although there can often be amazing similarities between members of a family group, only rarely are any two exactly the same. Offspring share certain characteristics with their parents, sisters, and brothers because they are all part of the same gene pool. That is, a proportion of their genes are the same.

Young may even resemble grandparents or more distant relatives. However, each offspring is unique owing to differences in its genetic makeup. The cells of any one individual have many thousands of different genes. Sometimes a particular gene controls a specific trait, such as eye color. But the

Children can look strikingly similar to their parents, sisters, and brothers, and sometimes even their grandparents. That is because they all share common genes.

situation is often much more complicated because many genes can work together on one trait.

Each gene can exist in a variety of different forms called alleles. Some alleles are dominant.

UNDERSTANDING ALLELES

Two alleles control wing case color in these beetles. One is dominant (R) and gives a red color; the other is recessive (r) and gives a black color. Only when an individual has two copies of the r allele does it have black wing cases.

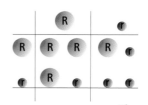

This table shows the combinations of genes that will occur in the young beetles.

There are three different combinations, resulting in two different wing case colors.

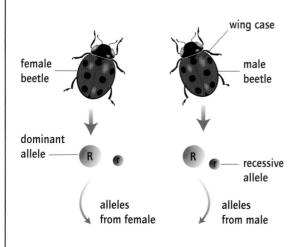

Double dominant alleles cause red wing case color.

One dominant and one recessive allele cause red wing case color.

One dominant and one recessive allele cause red wing case color.

Double recessive alleles cause black wing case color.

MULTIPLE BIRTHS

In most cases of twins the offspring develop separately, may be of either sex, and are no more similar at birth than ordinary sisters and brothers. However, there are rare occasions when, owing to the division of a single **zygote** (fertilized egg), each of the halves grows into a separate baby. These babies are genetically identical. They are of the same sex and similar in appearance and behavior. What do people call this type of twins?

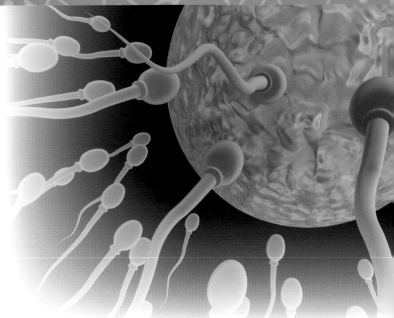

A new life begins when a tiny male sperm cell bursts through the membrane of a female egg cell. This is known as fertilization and ensures a good mix of genetic material.

They appear frequently in a group of organisms, and the properties they code for are always expressed. Other alleles are recessive. They are rare and are expressed only when there are no dominant alleles present.

Members of the same family group have the same sets of genes. However, they are likely to carry different combinations of alleles. These combinations make us differ from one another.

Recombination

When a new generation of offspring is produced, **sexual reproduction** results in a mixing of the different alleles. This allows entirely new combinations to be produced. This process, **recombination**, is caused in part by the effects of meiosis, a type of cell division in which sex cells (sperm and eggs) form. Fertilization, the fusion of a male and female sex cell, is also important. Each sex cell carries inside it half of the alleles of the future offspring.

Any population is made up of a number of breeding individuals. If the process of sexual reproduction shuffles the alleles each time, then the combinations of alleles across the whole population are also likely to change. This change in the genetic makeup at population level—from one generation to another—is the basis of evolution. Evolution is the

process of change that takes place as organisms adapt to their environment.

Since the characteristics of organisms are largely determined by their genes, evolution can bring about changes in the characteristics of populations through the generations. There are several different ways in which these evolutionary changes can take place, and they include mutation, natural and sexual selection, genetic drift, and migration.

Mutation

A mistake made when genes are replicated that leads to the appearance of entirely new genes is called a mutation. If the error in copying occurs when the sex cells are being formed, the mistake is then inherited by the offspring. The variety of alleles is the result of genetic mutations. Natural selection, genetic drift, and migration change the combinations of genes in a population, but these processes cannot create new ones. Mutations can have a positive effect (and increase through the population), a negative effect (populations die out), or a neutral effect (have no effect on the population unless conditions change).

Selection

Natural selection is a process by which those individuals in a population best adapted to an environment reproduce successfully, while those that are less able fail to do so. As a result, the population changes over time—it evolves. There are three forms of natural selection: directional, stabilizing, and disruptive. Directional selection favors more extreme forms of a feature. Individuals with extreme characteristics are more likely to survive than those with more average features. Selection can sometimes be stabilizing, favoring intermediate forms at the expense of extreme types.

Selection is described as disruptive when both extremes of a trait, such as the largest and smallest, survive at the expense of intermediates. This may occur during the formation of a new species. However, selection can occur only if variation between individuals has a genetic basis and can be inherited by young.

Genetic drift

There is another source of genetic variation that can occur during the production of sex cells. This process, genetic drift, is a change in how often alleles appear in a population through random chance. Genetic drift is not affected by natural selection, but it can still lead to evolutionary change. In large, stable populations the effects of genetic drift tend to be canceled out by the size of the gene pool—allele frequencies may vary a little but will generally tend to remain the same.

However, the effects of chance are more apparent in smaller populations. In a small population new generations are likely to have less genetic diversity than their parents. Genetic drift may result in alleles being lost. This leads to a characteristic becoming fixed. That is, both alleles that together form a gene are the same, so there is no variation. Once lost, the allele can only be reestablished through migration from elsewhere by individuals carrying the lost allele.

Subtle physical characteristics, such as the wing length of a bird, can be the deciding factor in natural selection.

SELECTING SPARROWS

In 1889, a fierce storm in the United States killed a number of house sparrows. The dead sparrows were found to be long- and short-winged individuals. Intermediate-winged sparrows survived. In this case selection favored average individuals. Which type of selection is operating here? Why has natural selection acted against the extreme forms of sparrows in this situation?

SELECTION OR DRIFT?

Since it is difficult to assess genetic drift outside the laboratory, scientists have been unable to present conclusive evidence of how much variation genetic drift causes in natural populations. To find out whether a characteristic results from natural selection or drift, they must first be able to figure out whether it is adaptive (gives an advantage) or not, and for many traits this is not usually possible.

The founder effect

Genetic drift also plays an important role in a phenomenon called the **founder effect**. It occurs when a small group of individuals becomes separated from the main population. This small founder group has only a fraction of the genetic variation present in the original gene pool because alleles are not spread evenly among individuals. Again, the genetic makeup of the group depends on chance. The frequency of rare alleles may be much higher in the founder group, so in future generations the rare allele may appear more frequently.

Without further mutations natural selection is limited to variation present in the founder group. Evolution is likely to follow a different course than that of the main population. Over time this may lead to speciation—the formation of a new species.

Migration and gene flow

When an individual leaves one population and joins another, it is said to migrate. Genes carried by a migrating individual are lost from one population through emigration and gained by the population it joins through immigration. Movement of genes between populations is called **gene flow**.

UNDERSTANDING GENETIC DRIFT AND FLOW

1. A diverse population of butterflies. Each colored spot represents a different form of an allele—two alleles together form a gene.
2. A female butterfly mates. Her young have one of two alleles of the gene. The butterfly is blown in a storm to a distant island, where she lays her eggs.
3. Due to random chance more young inherit the blue allele than the yellow allele, while those with the red allele do not survive to adulthood.
4. Through genetic drift the yellow allele is also lost. The island population now has very low genetic diversity.
5. A second female butterfly, containing eggs with a different combination of alleles, is blown from the original population to the island.
6. Through gene flow some of the diversity of the original population is restored to the island butterflies.

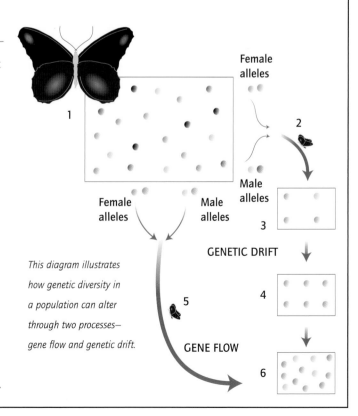

This diagram illustrates how genetic diversity in a population can alter through two processes—gene flow and genetic drift.

Gene flow continues as long as the populations do not become completely separated from one another, and migrating individuals can continue to interbreed and share their genes.

ISLAND EVOLUTION

Animals that evolve on islands often share some common features. Island birds such as kiwis are often flightless, though they had flying ancestors. With few or no predators to deal with, the birds evolved to walk and run instead. Small animals, such as tortoises, tend to become much larger on islands, while larger animals, such as deer and tigers, decrease in size to help cope with a limited food supply.

Around 10,000 years ago cheetahs underwent a dramatic population crash—perhaps just a single female and her cubs survived. This genetic bottleneck meant that cheetahs now have very little genetic diversity.

Genetic bottlenecks

Some species, such as the cheetah, have very little genetic variation. That is because population numbers decreased dramatically in the past. Among cheetahs this decline took place around 10,000 years ago. Cheetah numbers then recovered from a founder group, although there were no other cheetahs around. A dramatic decline in numbers with a corresponding crash in genetic diversity is called a **genetic bottleneck**.

Inbreeding

Founder effect can cause an increase in the frequency of recessive genes that can cause serious harm to an organism. That can also happen when closely related individuals mate. The decline in fitness (ability to survive and reproduce) that results from this is called inbreeding depression. It is particularly important for organisms that can potentially breed with themselves,

GENE FLOW IN CONSERVATION

Reducing a habitat into small patches separated from each other can have devastating effects for the species that live there. Without gene flow genetic diversity drops. Inbreeding can cause an increase in lethal genes.

Without patches of suitable habitat, or corridors, to link habitat fragments much of an area's biodiversity may be lost. Roads and highways are a major barrier to gene flow for some species. However, artificial corridors linking fragments can sometimes be set up. In some parts of Europe dormice are able to cross roads by using a network of ropes that act as corridors.

The genetic diversity of the giant panda has suffered thanks to a loss of habitat.

such as plants. Not all plants avoid inbreeding. It is a way to ensure that at least some seeds will form. However, it also leads to low genetic diversity. For most types of plants, breeding with other individuals is essential.

HUMAN GENETIC BOTTLENECK

Cheetahs are not the only animals to have very little genetic diversity. You might be surprised to know that humans are also among the least genetically diverse of all creatures. Scientists think that is because humans almost became extinct around 70,000 years ago, perhaps due to famine or disease. The global population around this time may have fallen as low as 2,000. This collapse in numbers led to a major decrease in genetic diversity, or a bottleneck. From this low point the human population slowly began to increase. Every person alive today is a descendent of this tiny band of ancient survivors.

Turnip flowers have male parts that release pollen and female parts that contain eggs. Pollen is carried by insects between flowers. On the outside of each turnip pollen grain are molecules called ligands. Their structure is genetically controlled. In part of the female flower called the stigma these same genes control the shape of molecules called kinases. If a pollen grain from one plant lands on a stigma of another, it grows a tube through the stigma to reach the eggs inside. Sperm moves through the tube to the eggs to form seeds. But if a pollen grain lands on a stigma of the same plant, the ligands on the pollen bind with the kinases. The pollen grain does not grow the tube to the eggs, and inbreeding is avoided.

Rates of evolution

Biologists know that evolution takes place, but at what speed? There are several main theories, but biologists are unsure which is correct. At first, it was thought that evolution was a process of gradual change. Biologists argued that small changes in an organism's structure led to a gradual divergence and the formation of new species over millions of years.

The golden lion tamarin population has recovered following conservation efforts.

MINIMUM VIABLE POPULATION

In conserving an endangered species, scientists need to figure out the **minimum viable population**, or MVP. This figure is the smallest possible population that could survive, with a degree of certainty, for a set period (usually 500 years) without harmful levels of inbreeding or genetic drift. The golden lion tamarin was once one of the world's most endangered primates. Thirty years ago there were only about 100 individuals left in the wild. They live only in the Atlantic rain forests of Brazil, where their habitat has been almost totally destroyed by human activities such tree logging. The MVP of this species is around 2,000. Conservationists have worked hard to establish zoo populations, and some captive-bred animals have been released into the wild.

Later, scientists suggested that the rate of evolution varied, and changes in the structures of fossils could be explained by rapid evolution and extreme directional natural selection. Periods with fossils of similar structures suggested times of evolutionary stability.

Punctuated equilibria

U.S. biologists Niles Eldredge (born 1943) and Stephen Jay Gould (1941–2002) proposed another model of evolution, which they called "punctuated equilibria," in 1972. They suggested that new species formed rapidly, and this speciation took place in small areas. Intermediate forms do not show up often in the fossil record as a result. These new species then move from the point of species formation and spread to new areas.

The theory of punctuated equilibria is only accepted in part by biologists today. The rate of evolution remains an issue of considerable debate.

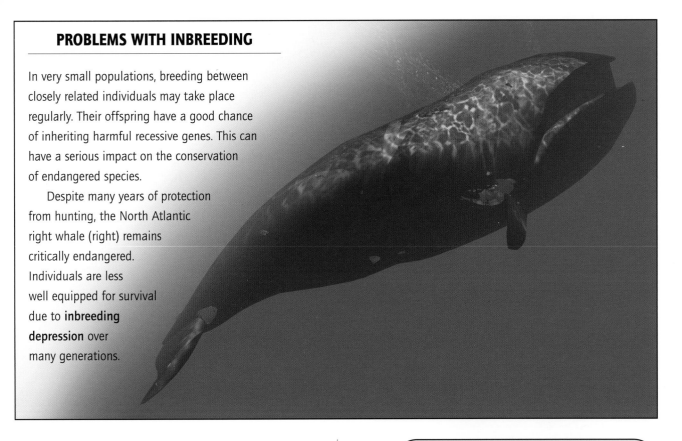

PROBLEMS WITH INBREEDING

In very small populations, breeding between closely related individuals may take place regularly. Their offspring have a good chance of inheriting harmful recessive genes. This can have a serious impact on the conservation of endangered species.

Despite many years of protection from hunting, the North Atlantic right whale (right) remains critically endangered. Individuals are less well equipped for survival due to **inbreeding depression** over many generations.

A molecular approach

Scientists first estimated evolutionary rates by looking at the age of fossils and their structures. In the 1960s Japanese biologist Motoo Kimura (1924–1994) proposed the neutral theory of molecular evolution. It provided a new dating system and changed the way biologists studied evolutionary history.

Kimura suggested that most mutations are neutral—they are neither beneficial or harmful. Neutral mutations build up in the genome (an organism's entire genetic material) at a constant rate. The mutations then spread through the population by gene flow.

Despite the genetic basis of evolution being relatively well understood for many years now, scientists have only recently measured evolutionary rates using molecular studies. Before Kimura's research biologists had to rely on just the fossil record, which is incomplete.

SCIENCE WORDS

- **founder effect** Phenomenon that causes low genetic diversity and unusual genes to be expressed in populations (such as those on islands) founded by just a few individuals.
- **inbreeding depression** Lack of fitness due to inbreeding and the buildup of recessive genes.
- **minimum viable population (MVP)** The smallest possible population a species can tolerate before extinction becomes inevitable.
- **recombination** The shuffling of genes during sexual reproduction. It leads to increased genetic diversity.
- **sexual reproduction** Production of young through the fusion of sex cells, often after mating between a male and a female.
- **zygote** An egg fertilized by a sperm that will develop into a new organism.

PATTERNS IN EVOLUTION

Understanding what species are and the different ways they can form allows biologists to chart patterns in evolution over time.

Renowned for their strength and stubbornness, mules are hybrids of male donkeys and female horses.

Populations of animals and plants alter over long periods of time through natural selection, mutation, and genetic drift. This change, or evolution, leads to a fine-tuning of an organism's adaptation to its environment. Splits in a population lead to speciation. This is the formation of a new species. The species is the basic unit of biological **classification**, the system used by biologists to organize their understanding of the natural world. But what exactly is a species?

Species concepts

The answer to this question may seem simple, but it is far from straightforward. The term species can be defined in several ways, but none encompasses all forms of life past and present. The most commonly used definition is "a group of organisms that can interbreed only with each other." This is known as the biological species concept.

There are, however, major problems with this definition. It only applies to organisms that reproduce sexually through the fusion of sperm and egg. Creatures that proliferate by **asexual reproduction**, such as most bacteria, are

---

WHAT'S IN A NAME?

In 1758, Swedish naturalist Carolus Linnaeus (1707–1778) introduced a classification system that is still used today. Linnaeus gave each species a pair of scientific names in Latin. The first, which always has a capital letter, is the name of the genus, a group of closely related organisms. Humans belong to the genus *Homo*.

The second part of the name refers only to the species. In humans it is *sapiens*, so the full name is *Homo sapiens*. This classification system allows biologists to understand the evolutionary history of a species, since closely related species share the same genus name.

SUBDIVIDING SPECIES

Populations within a species can differ from one another while still being able to interbreed. These populations are known as subspecies. Subspecies often occupy a particular geographic range, and they may have subtle differences of color or behavior. For example, Rothschild's giraffe lives in East Africa and can be clearly distinguished from other giraffes by the color of its and the lack of patterning on its lower legs.

Subspecies are very important to scientists trying to understand how speciation works. The subspecies represent an intermediate stage between an ancestral population and a completely new species.

Today, biologists often use a different definition for the word species. Called the evolutionary species concept, it states that a species consists of individuals that share the same evolutionary history. This includes asexual organisms, but can be difficult to extend to fossil groups.

Cryptic species complex

Some species look, to human eyes, identical to others. They can only be distinguished by detailed behavioral or genetic studies. Biologists call them

excluded. Fossil organisms, too, do not fall within this definition of a species.

Also, mating between different species can sometimes occur in nature. The young of such interspecies pairings are called hybrids. They are often sterile and unable to successfully reproduce; but for some groups, such as certain plants, hybridization can be an essential step in the formation of a new species.

There are more than 100 species of evening primrose, many of which can interbreed to produce hybrids.

cryptic species complex. They seem to be surprisingly common, and may be the cause of a major underestimate of Earth's biodiversity.

One of the best-known discoveries of a cryptic species complex concerned the pipistrelle bat, which lives in Europe. Bats find their way around in the dark by emitting high-pitched squeaks and then listening to the echoes from their surroundings. In the 1990s, a group of English biologists noticed that some pipistrelles squeaked at a much higher frequency than others, although there were no anatomical differences between the bats.

Following up this hunch, the biologists looked at the genes of the bats. They found that the bats actually formed two separate species. Today, the one with the higher-frequency calls is known as the soprano pipistrelle.

Biologists do not, at present, precisely understand how cryptic species evolve. However, their speciation is probably sympatric (see below).

How do new species form?

Species arise when an existing species diverges. This can happen in different ways. One process, called **allopatric speciation**, takes place when a population is split by a geographical barrier. The barrier may be a river or a mountain chain. Allopatric speciation also occurs when organisms reach an offshore island and are separated from the rest of the population.

During allopatric speciation the two populations evolve until individuals from one are unable to breed with individuals from the other.

A different type of speciation, **sympatric speciation**, does not require geographical barriers. It occurs when a species diverges (splits) to avoid competition or make use of a new food source.

Sympatric speciation can also take place through hybridization. For many organisms a difference in the number of chromosomes (packages of genes) means breeding cannot take place between different

Pipistrelle bats are an example of a cryptic species complex—different species may look identical but the frequency of their echolocation calls separated them out as different species.

species. This does not affect some plants, though. Instead, these species simply double up the number of chromosomes they have during reproduction. This is called polyploidy, and it results in very fast speciation that happens in a single generation. This is important in the production of new crop strains. *Triticum aestivum,* for example, is a type of wheat that has six times as many chromosomes as its wild ancestors. Polyploid plants usually have fleshier leaves and larger seeds than plants with normal chromosome numbers.

Reproductive isolation

Regardless of the mechanism, speciation depends on the individuals of one population being unable to breed with individuals from the other. Biologists call this **reproductive isolation**. It stops gene flow, which may act to cancel out each population's adaptations.

The barriers to reproduction may be geographical if two species become adapted to different habitats. There may also be time-related barriers. Different species may be active at different times of day, or they may breed at different times of the year. This is the case for many species of plants.

After speciation has taken place, mechanisms remain to help avoid breeding between members of the two species. That is because any young produced would be hybrids, which are usually less well adapted to the environment than either parent species.

Wheat is an example of a polyploid crop. Some wheat species have four sets of chromosomes (tetraploid), while others have six (hexaploid).

VIGOROUS HYBRIDS

The existence of hybrids creates big problems for the biological species concept. Most hybrids are poorly adapted to survive, and they are often unable to breed. But sometimes hybrids of closely related species may be better equipped to survive than either of their parents. This is called hybrid vigor, and it especially applies to plants. Many crops, such as corn, are crosses cultivated to exploit hybrid vigor.

ANT-EATING ANIMALS

There are many mammals that feed on ants and termites. Some have developed long noses and tongues to smell out and gather up the insects, and have powerful front limbs to tear open the insects' nests. The aardvark from South Africa is one such animal. Can you think of another animal from another part of the world that has developed the same sort of adaptations to its lifestyle?

Native to Australia, the egg-laying echidna, or spiny anteater, eats mainly ants and termites and shares a similar lifestyle to other insect-eating mammals such as the true anteaters of South America.

Adaptive radiation

Within any environment are many niches. They are the different lifestyles and habitats of organisms. The akiapola'au (a type of finch), for example, fills the niche of insect catcher on Hawaiian trees. A species in an area with vacant niches will diverge to fill them. Each generation will become better adapted to a particular niche, and new species form. Biologists call this process adaptive radiation.

The Galápagos Islands in the Pacific Ocean are well known for their 14 species of finches. These finches share a common ancestor that flew to the islands from South America. In the absence of competitors the finches radiated, and new species swiftly formed. Each finch species evolved a different beak shape. These shapes were related to the niches and food sources to which each new species was adapted.

Coevolution

Sometimes the evolution of two or more species is closely tied together. This is called **coevolution**. Some organisms have evolved such a close relationship with one another that they cannot exist in isolation. Ruminants include animals such

ADAPTIVE RADIATION

Honeycreepers diverged into many new species on the Hawaiian Islands over many millions of years in much the same way as the finches that are found on the Galápagos Islands.

Through adaptive radiation honeycreepers evolved into new niches and exploited different food sources. Their beaks changed shape dramatically to suit their foods. Some have thick beaks, suited to eating insects, seeds, and fruits. Others have slender, downcurved beeks for sipping nectar.

Most species of honeycreepers are critically endangered, and some are now extinct.

as cattle, sheep, goats, and deer. They are unable to digest cellulose, a tough chemical found in plants, but ruminants need the energy it contains.

Ruminants depend on the microorganisms that live in their guts. The microorganisms break down the cellulose in the food eaten by the ruminant, making it easier to digest. In return, the ruminants provide a safe, warm environment with unlimited food for their tiny internal partners. Neither the ruminants nor the microorganisms could survive without the other. A close relationship like this, in which both partners benefit, is called a mutualism. It results from millions of years of coevolution.

However, coevolution does not always result in mutual benefit. For example, predators and their prey are involved in a biological "arms race." As predators evolve and become increasingly successful at hunting, their prey also evolve better ways of escaping capture.

Convergent evolution

Organisms that are not closely related can evolve similar anatomies in response to living in similar environments. This is called convergent evolution.

Many Australian marsupials are convergent with mammals from other parts of the world. For example,

---

RADIATION AND REPLACEMENT

On rare occasions during Earth's history a group has evolved a dramatic evolutionary advantage that allowed it to sweep away the competition. One of these episodes was the evolution of the amniote egg (right) in an ancient amphibian group around 300 million years ago. Amniote eggs had waterproof shells. They allowed the animals to lay eggs far from water. Allied with a waterproof skin, the amniote egg allowed this new animal group, the reptiles, to move into niches that were unavailable to amphibians. This triggered rapid speciation through adaptive radiation. With their better adaptations for life away from water reptiles soon replaced amphibians as the dominant land vertebrates. Later reptiles diverged into two other major amniote groups; mammals and birds.

The structure of an amniote egg, as found today in reptiles, birds, and a few mammals. The amnion and chorion are membranes that control the movement of water and oxygen. Most mammals, including humans, have a modified form of this egg inside the uterus.

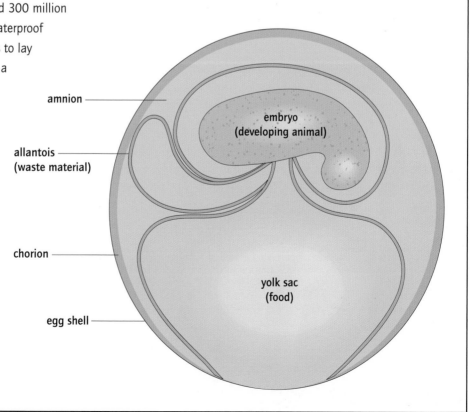

amnion

embryo (developing animal)

allantois (waste material)

chorion

yolk sac (food)

egg shell

there is a burrowing marsupial that looks just like a mole. There is a gliding marsupial that is very similar to a flying squirrel, and even a marsupial "cat," the quoll, that looks and acts like a domestic cat.

Convergence over time

Convergent evolution does not have to take place at the same time. Study of the fossil record shows that certain body patterns, or ectomorphs, have evolved again and again in different animals groups.

Biologists call this **iterative evolution**. A good example is the wide range of saber-toothed mammals.

Saber-toothed mammals used their long canine teeth to help them kill large prey quickly. The earliest saber-tooths belonged to a group of mammals called the creodonts, which lived around 50 million years ago. Later, saber teeth evolved twice among the carnivores, first in the extinct, catlike nimravids, then in the true cats themselves. The last of these saber-toothed cats, *Smilodon,* lived in North America and died out only around 11,000 years ago.

Marsupial saber-tooths

Saber teeth also evolved among marsupial mammals. *Thylacosmilus* was a leopardlike animal that lived in South America until around 2 million years ago. *Thylacosmilus* had truly enormous canine teeth. These teeth rested within a pair of flanges that extended down from the lower jaw. The canines of this fearsome beast continued to grow throughout its life. The flanges helped wear the teeth down and kept them sharp.

Cows rely on gut bacteria to break down the tough cellulose in their plant food. Both the cows and the bacteria benefit from the close relationship, which is known as mutualism.

ANTIPREDATOR MEASURES

In order to survive, prey animals have developed a wide range of adaptations that help them locate and escape from predatory animals. Ungulates, for example, are hoofed mammals, many of which are plant-eaters that live on grasslands. Most ungulates live in herds. That is because many eyes are better at spotting potential predators than just a single pair. Can you think of any other antipredator adaptations that these animals share?

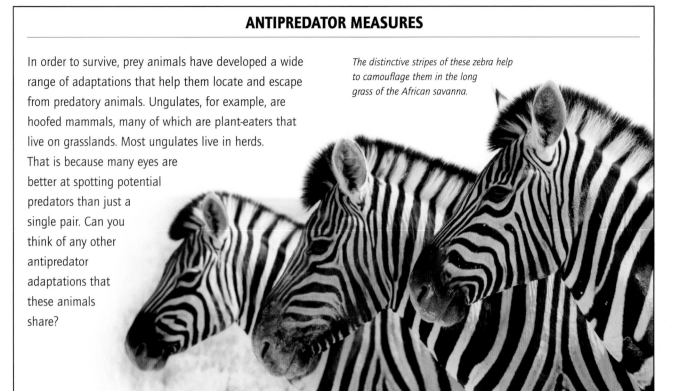

The distinctive stripes of these zebra help to camouflage them in the long grass of the African savanna.

There are no saber-toothed mammals today, but the clouded leopard from central Asia has, relatively, the largest canines of any cat. Maybe over the next million years or so, descendants of this forest leopard will evolve true saber teeth.

Extinctions

More than 99 percent of all the species that have ever existed are now extinct. The average "lifespan" of a species (time between species formation and extinction) is 2 to 3 million years, although some, such as horseshoe crabs, have changed very little over much longer periods of time.

Extinction can be caused by climate or habitat changes, the effects of competing organisms, and volcanoes or meteor impacts. At times in Earth's history large numbers of species have died out in a short space of time. Biologists call them **mass extinctions**. For example, a mass extinction saw the end of the dinosaurs 65 million years ago.

SCIENCE WORDS

- **allopatric speciation** The formation of new species through geographic isolation.
- **coevolution** Evolution involving changes in two species that depend on each other to survive.
- **cryptic species complex** Species that are indistinguishable from one another without genetic study.
- **iterative evolution** Repeated evolution of similar structures in different groups over long periods of time.
- **reproductive isolation** The separation of one population from another so they cannot interbreed.
- **sympatric speciation** The formation of new species through behavioral and other mechanisms rather than geographic isolation.

THE STORY OF LIFE

Scientists believe the first simple life-forms evolved in the oceans around 3.8 billion years ago. More than 3 billion years later plants and animals first moved from the waters onto Earth's dry land.

Around 4.5 billion years ago the newly formed Earth was a lifeless ball of molten rock. Volcanoes erupted, releasing gases that formed an atmosphere. It was different from the atmosphere of today, since it did not contain oxygen but poisonous gases. The water vapor gradually cooled to form the oceans, where life began around 3.8 billion years ago.

GEOLOGICAL TIME

Biologists divide Earth's history into huge eras, which are separated into periods. The order of periods was determined by looking at the fossils contained in the rocks. By analyzing how radioactive minerals decay in rocks from each period, scientists can estimate the time (shown here in millions of years) since each period occurred.

Coral reefs are home to an amazing biodiversity.

Era	Age	Geological time period		First appearance
Tertiary (Phanerozoic)	2	PLEISTOCENE		hominids (Pliocene)
	5	PLIOCENE		apes (Miocene)
	11	MIOCENE	Upper	
	16		Middle	monkeys (Oligocene)
	24		Lower	horses (Eocene)
	37	OLIGOCENE		
	58	EOCENE		
	65	PALEOCENE		
Mesozoic (Phanerozoic)	97	CRETACEOUS	Upper	modern mammals (Cretaceous)
	144		Lower	flowering plants (Cretaceous)
		JURASSIC	Upper	birds (Jurassic)
			Middle	dinosaurs (Triassic)
	208		Lower	
	245	TRIASSIC	Upper	
			Middle	
			LOWER	
Paleozoic (Phanerozoic)	286	PERMIAN	UPPER	reptiles (Permian)
			Lower	
	360	CARBONIFEROUS	Upper	amphibians (Devonian)
			Lower	sharks (Devonian)
		DEVONIAN	Upper	ammonoids (Silurian)
	408		Middle	jawed fish (Silurian)
			Lower	land plants (Ordovician)
	438	SILURIAN	Upper	trilobites (Cambrian)
			MIDDLE	
			Lower	
	505	ORDOVICIAN	Upper	
			Middle	
			Lower	
	570	CAMBRIAN	Upper	
			Middle	
			Lower	
Precambrian	900	PROTEROZOIC	Upper	soft-bodied animals (Proterozoic)
	1,600		Middle	oldest deposits from glaciers (Archean)
	2,500		Lower	
	4,600	ARCHEAN		

The earliest known life-forms were tiny, single-celled organisms called **prokaryotes**, such as bacteria. Some, called cyanobacteria, used the energy from sunlight to make food, releasing oxygen in the process. The oxygen formed a layer of ozone gas high in Earth's atmosphere, which blocked many of the Sun's harmful ultraviolet rays. The buildup of oxygen killed off many ancient prokaryote groups, but the survivors were able to use oxygen to produce energy from food efficiently.

"Cradle of Life"

Biologists are divided over the type of environment in which life first appeared on Earth. Some believe life began within an ice-covered ocean. Others think it happened in the boiling cauldron of a hydrothermal vent on the seabed. Yet other experts believe that life began in shallow tidal pools fed by minerals from geysers and volcanoes. Meteors and comets that crashed onto the young Earth's surface may also have helped supply the raw materials needed before life could begin.

More complex life

Around 1.8 billion years ago more advanced organisms called **eukaryotes** evolved. Unlike prokaryotes, these single-celled organisms had genetic material contained within a nuclear membrane. The first eukaryotes formed through the union of two different prokaryotes that lived together for mutual benefit. One of these once-free organisms now forms the mitochondria, miniorgans in cells that provide energy.

Metazoan life

Millions of years later metazoans, organisms consisting of many cells, appeared. Cells were organized into tissues specialized for feeding, moving, and reproducing. One of the oldest metazoan fossils known is the trail left by a wormlike animal as it burrowed through the mud more than 1 billion years ago.

These ancient soft-bodied metazoans included worms and jellyfish. They are called ediacarans, after the Ediacara Hills in Australia, which contain a famous deposit of fossils from this time. Most of the phyla, or large groups, of animals with shells and other hard body parts appeared during a period called the Cambrian explosion, about 535 million years ago. Important groups such as the mollusks, echinoderms (starfish and relatives), and arthropods (which today include spiders and insects) appeared around this time.

Volcanic eruptions that occurred billions of years ago pumped gases into the air, helping form the atmosphere on which life on Earth depends.

TRY THIS

Fossil Imprints

Ediacaran organisms are known only from the imprints that their bodies made in soft mud or trace fossils such as burrows and tracks. Experts use these clues to try to figure out what the creatures looked like. They test their theories by making models that create similar prints.

You can carry out similar experiments by making imprints of natural objects such such as leaves or pinecones in wet clay. Then get your friends to try to guess what made the prints.

This is a fossil of an organism known as an ammonite. These spiral-shaped invertebrates lived in the oceans between 240 and 65 million years ago. The modern relatives of ammonites include cuttlefish, octopuses, and squid.

The first vertebrates

Around 450 million years ago the first vertebrates (backboned creatures) developed. They were jawless fish similar to modern lampreys. Later, in Devonian times some types of lobe-finned fish evolved lunglike pouches to breathe air and sturdy fins to heave themselves along the bottom. Fish like these began to crawl onto the shore, perhaps to escape competition with other fish or to feed. They joined plants and animals, such as insects and spiders, that had already colonized the land.

These ancient fish evolved into amphibians. Although they could move and breathe on land, they quickly lost water through their skins and had to return to water to breed. With the evolution of the amniote, or shelled, egg, around 330 million years ago a new group of vertebrates with waterproof skins, the reptiles, displaced the amphibians as the main land vertebrates.

The age of reptiles

Since they could live and lay eggs far from water, reptiles were able to colonize many new habitats.

Early reptiles looked like small lizards; but after the Permian mass extinction reptiles came to dominate the land, sea, and sky.

Marine reptiles such as the long-necked plesiosaurs, the mosasaurs, and the dolphin-like ichthyosaurs swam in the oceans along with fish, crustaceans such as crabs and lobsters, and mollusks such as ammonites and squids. Flying reptiles called pterosaurs skimmed through the air on skin-covered wings. The largest and most spectacular reptile group, the dinosaurs, lived on land along with insects, amphibians, early mammals, and birds. With the evolution of flowering plants around 100 million years ago insects flourished, and new groups such as bees appeared.

MASS EXTINCTIONS

Throughout Earth's history organisms have evolved, flourished, and died out. Sometimes vast numbers of species die out around the same time. This is called a mass extinction. The causes of mass extinctions are hard to pinpoint. Some may have been caused by asteroid impacts or volcanic eruptions that blocked out the Sun.

The greatest mass extinction occurred at the end of the Permian period, 245 million years ago, when up to 95 percent of all life on Earth became extinct. Scientists think mass extinctions occur in cycles. They happen, on average, once every 26 million years.

Dinosaur diversity

More than 1,000 different dinosaur species have been identified from fossils. Some were small, chicken-sized animals, but others, such as long-necked sauropod dinosaurs like *Diplodocus,* were as big as jet liners. Biologists can tell a lot about how dinosaurs lived by looking at their bones. The structure of dinosaur teeth reveals that many dinosaurs, including the sauropods, stegosaurs, ankylosaurs, and ceratopsians such as *Triceratops*, ate plant material. Others were predatory meat eaters. One of the biggest and best known, *Tyrannosaurus rex*, was a solitary hunter; but smaller, nimbler predators such as coelurosaurs are thought to have hunted in packs.

Hot dinosaurs?

After many years of debate scientists are now sure that unlike living reptiles, dinosaurs were warm-blooded and did not rely on their surroundings for temperature control. Sauropods were large enough to retain their heat permanently. Smaller species produced their own heat to stay warm. Stunning fossil finds were made in China in the 1990s of dinosaurs with plumages of fine, downy feathers that kept them warm. Some pterosaurs also had hairs on their bodies to retain heat. The presence of feathers on dinosaurs resolved another long-running debate. It proved that birds, like the sparrows on your bird feeder, descend from dinosaurs.

HOW MANY DIGITS?

Take a close look at your fingers. In your very distant ancestors these bones formed the rays of a fin. After these lobe-finned fish invaded the land, the rays became digits. Scientists were surprised to find that early land vertebrates had up to 8 digits rather than the 5 found today. The extra digits were lost soon after the invasion of the land. Also, check out how the bones in your arm and hand have evolved over millions of years.

radius
humerus
ulna
rays and digits
palm bones

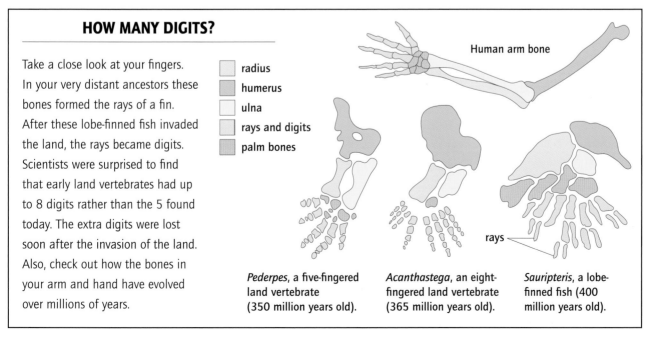

Human arm bone

rays

Pederpes, a five-fingered land vertebrate (350 million years old).

Acanthastega, an eight-fingered land vertebrate (365 million years old).

Sauripteris, a lobe-finned fish (400 million years old).

WHY DID THE DINOSAURS GROW SO BIG?

Huge, plant-eating sauropod dinosaurs such as *Diplodocus* and *Brachiosaurus* were far bigger than the largest land animal of today, the African bush elephant. These giants evolved long necks that helped them browse among the treetops and spot danger from afar. When predatory dinosaurs also grew large, only the biggest individual sauropods survived to pass on their genes. This **biological arms race** drove the evolution of ever-larger sauropods, culminating in *Argentinosaurus,* which may have weighed more than 100 tons (90 t)!

Becoming birds

Birds evolved from small dinosaurs around 170 million years ago. The feathers that dinosaurs used to keep warm were modified for flight. The discovery in 2003 of a gliding dinosaur with four wings, one on each leg, strongly suggests that birds developed from dinosaurs adapted for climbing that glided from tree to tree. Ancient birds retained several reptilian characteristics not present in modern birds. *Archaeopteryx*, for example, had a long, bony tail, teeth, and claws on its wings.

Mammal beginnings

Another major vertebrate group, mammals, had evolved from reptiles slightly earlier, around 210 million years ago. Mammals developed from a group of mammal-like reptiles called cynodonts. While dinosaurs dominated the land, these warm-blooded, furry creatures remained small and ratlike.

Around 65 million years ago a mysterious disaster led to the extinction of the dinosaurs, along with the pterosaurs, most of the marine reptiles, and several other groups such as the ammonites. Smaller reptiles, such as lizards, turtles, and crocodiles, survived, along with amphibians, mammals, and birds, and invertebrate groups such as spiders and insects. The extinction of the dinosaurs allowed mammals to grow larger, and soon they became the dominant vertebrates on land and in the sea.

Mammals everywhere

On land the mammals quickly diversified. In the northern hemisphere the first horses, camels, elephants, monkeys, and rodents appeared, along with the forerunners of carnivores such as wolves, bears, and cats. They were all placental mammals. Their young developed inside their mothers

The ancestors of the modern dolphin evolved about 10 million years ago, during a period in Earth's history called the Miocene epoch.

The alligator is a "living fossil." It has changed very little since the first alligators appeared on Earth, around 230 million years ago.

and were born well developed. In South America, Australia, and Antarctica a different group, the marsupials, flourished. Their young were born tiny and helpless, and developed inside a pouch on the mother's body. Just a few mammals, such as the spiny anteaters, revealed their reptile origins by continuing to lay eggs.

DINOSAUR MIMICS

Ichthyosaurs were marine reptiles with extremely powerful, streamlined bodies ending in a forked tail. They had two front flippers for steering and long, narrow jaws lined with sharp teeth for catching prey. Unlike other reptile groups that laid eggs on land, ichthyosaurs gave birth to live young in the water.

In all these ways these speedy swimmers closely resembled modern dolphins, which are marine mammals; but the two groups are only distantly related. This is an example of convergent evolution, in which different groups evolve along similar lines to suit the type of environment in which they all live.

By around 50 million years ago bats flew in the night sky. Bats had a dramatic effect on moths and other nighttime insects. So severe was their predation that one group of moths gave up nocturnal life altogether and switched to the daytime. These insects became modern butterflies.

By the Miocene hoofed mammals such as deer and pigs thrived, while rodents diversified to become the largest of mammal groups. Being warm-blooded helped mammals survive climatic changes during the Pliocene, when long, cold periods called ice ages were interspersed with warmer spells.

SCIENCE WORDS

- **biological arms race** The coevolution of predators and their prey.
- **eukaryote** Cell containing organelles; animals, plants, and fungi are eukaryotes.
- **prokaryote** Single-celled organism, such as a bacterium, that does not contain miniorgans.

HUMAN EVOLUTION

Humans started to evolve from apelike ancestors more than five million years ago. Gradually, humans became skillful tool users, invented language, and spread across the world.

Charles Darwin was the first person to hint that humans had evolved over millions of years from apelike creatures. Darwin's views caused outrage and provoked ridicule. However, most people today accept the idea of human evolution. The theory is backed up by finds of fossil bones, ancient tools, and trackways, and through analysis of human and ape DNA.

The group from which humans descend split from the ancestors of modern apes around 5.5 million years ago, although fossils found in Chad in 2002 may push this figure back to 7 million years ago. Either way, the two groups evolved along separate lines. Humans' ape ancestors lived in forest trees, probably in East Africa. Around 5 million years ago the forerunners of humans moved from the trees to the ground, perhaps after a decline in forests due to climate change. They began to walk upright, freeing their hands for other tasks.

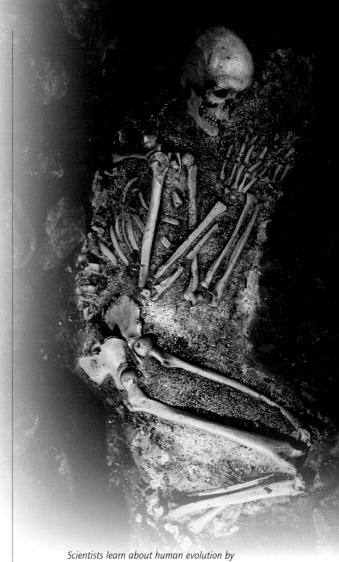

Scientists learn about human evolution by studying the fossil remains that have been found.

DNA EVIDENCE

In recent years, scientists have carried out DNA tests on humans and primates that show that people are closely related to apes such as chimpanzees and gorillas. Our closest living relatives are bonobos (left), which live in declining numbers in West Africa. This DNA evidence is supported by other scientific studies comparing the blood, brains, and other physical structures of humans, monkeys, and apes.

AFRICAN FINDS

Fossils of human ancestors such as the **Australopithecines** and *Homo habilis* come from eastern and southern Africa, where many hominid species, including our own, evolved. The rocks of the Great Rift Valley contain many vital clues about human evolution. In 1964 British paleontologists Louis (1903–1972) and Mary (1913–1996) Leakey found remains of *Homo habilis* at Olduvai Gorge in Tanzania. Many other remains were found in the gorge. Ethiopia is also rich with unique fossils. In 1974, U.S. paleontologist Don Johanson (born 1943) found a skeleton of *Australopithecus afarensis* at Hadar in Ethiopia. He named the soon-to-be-famous skeleton "Lucy."

Olduvai Gorge in the Great Rift Valley, Tanzania, is the site of many famous hominid fossil finds and stone-tool assemblages.

These prehumans, which together with their human descendants are known as **hominids**, began to evolve bigger brains. The earliest recognizably humanlike creatures lived 4 million years ago. They belong to a genus called *Australopithecus*, which means "southern ape," since their fossils were first found in southern Africa.

Human ancestors

Australopithecines lived in eastern and southern Africa between four and two million years ago. They looked like apes, but they walked upright as they wandered the plains in search of fruit, nuts, and roots. They were smaller than modern humans, with brains about one-third the size of ours. Several different types of australopithecines have been identified so far. They include the slender, slightly built species *Australopithecus afarensis*, which was discovered in Ethiopia in 1974. The first specimen found was a female nicknamed "Lucy."

Lucy was small, less than 4 feet (120 cm) tall. She had a chimp-sized brain and long, apelike arms, but she stood and walked upright. Many paleontologists think that humans are descended from a closely related species called *Australopithecus garhi*. This species was also discovered in Ethiopia in 1999.

FABULOUS FORGERY

Once Darwin's views became widely accepted, scientists searched hard for a "missing link." This halfway stage between apes and humans would prove that humans had evolved from apes. In 1915, an apelike human skull was found in a quarry in Piltdown, England. Piltdown Man was soon hailed as the missing link. For 40 years the authenticity of Piltdown man was unquestioned, but tests in 1953 showed it was a hoax, made by combining human and ape remains. No one knows who carried out this famous forgery.

APELIKE ANCESTORS

The first chapters of the Bible state that God created humans in His image and set them above all other animals. In the mid-19th century Christians took these words literally, so Darwin's suggestion that humans had evolved from more primitive creatures caused an uproar. Most people thought Darwin was saying that humans were descended from monkeys, but that was a misunderstanding.

Darwin realized that humans and apes shared a common ancestor in the distant past, but that apes have also continued to evolve. However, many people at the time thought that Darwin's ideas were ridiculous.

Handy humans

By two million years ago early humanlike hominids had evolved from one of the australopithecines. The first recognizably human species, which belonged to the genus *Homo* just as modern humans do, was *Homo habilis* (meaning "handy human"). Remains of this human ancestor have been found in Kenya and Tanzania in East Africa. Studies of the fossils show that *Homo habilis* was taller than any australopithecine, with a less jutting jaw and a brain around half the size of a modern human's. "Handy humans" are so-called because they were the first to fashion rough stone tools for cutting and scraping. Animal bones found in their camps bear scratches made by the stone

This stone arrowhead was found in Olduvai Gorge, Tanzania, Africa. It was made around 3 million years ago by a human ancestor called Homo habilis.

tools of our ancestors. No one can be sure whether these early humans actively hunted animals for food or simply scavenged meat they found from the kills of other predators.

Upright humans

By about 1.8 million years ago *Homo habilis* had evolved into several different species. Once they were lumped into a single species called *Homo erectus,* or "upright human"; but today they are split into several species, including *Homo heidelbergensis* and *Homo ergaster.* These hominids again originated in Africa but later migrated to settle in distant regions such as Europe, China, and, by around 1 million years ago, Indonesia. *Erectus*-like hominids were taller and faster than earlier species. Their brains increased in size over many thousands of generations until they were only a little smaller than that of modern humans. Scientists believe these early humans were

TRY THIS

Making Casts of Tracks

Scientists make casts of fossilized tracks, like the prints found at Laetoli, using plaster of Paris. Try making a cast of an animal track or even your own footprint in wet mud or sand using the same technique. First, make a ring of heavy paper, and put it around the print. Then mix the plaster of Paris with the water in a bowl. Once you have a thick plaster of Paris mixture, pour it onto the print, wait 20 minutes, and then lift it free. When the cast is quite hard about a day later, you can clean and decorate it if you like.

the first to make fire and to fashion clothing from animal skins to help them keep warm during the harsh winter weather.

Wise humans

By around 250,000 years ago one of these hominids (probably *Homo heidelbergensis*) had evolved into *Homo sapiens*—our own species—meaning "wise human." By 130,000 years ago modern humans, which belong to the subspecies *Homo sapiens sapiens*, had evolved in East Africa. All the people alive in the world today descend from these ancient folk.

There were other human subspecies around at this time, though. *Homo sapiens neanderthalensis*, or **Neanderthal** people, had short, burly bodies and lacked a chin. Neanderthals lived in Europe and the Middle East from around 130,000 years ago. They were skilled toolmakers and expert hunters—and the

SEXUAL DIMORPHISM

There is a marked difference in size between males and females in ancient hominids such as *Homo habilis*. Males of this species reached about 5 feet (1.5 m) tall, while

Although there is some sexual dimorphism in modern humans, it is less marked than in our hominid ancestors.

females were only 3 to 4 feet (90 to 120 cm) tall.

This difference, called sexual dimorphism, is also seen in apes such as gorillas as well as many other animal species. It became less marked in hominids by about 1 million years ago and is only slight in modern humans.

first people to bury their dead. Neanderthals died out around 30,000 years ago, at about the same time that *Homo sapiens sapiens* began to make rapid technological and cultural strides.

The spread of humans

Around 100,000 years ago modern humans began to spread from Africa to other parts of the world. People had reached distant Australia by 60,000 years ago. By 30,000 years ago people had colonized northern Asia. Their descendants, around 20,000 years ago, crossed into North America via a land bridge through the Bering Strait. These people then quickly spread south through Central and South America.

The birth of civilization

Between 40,000 and 10,000 years ago a group of modern humans called Cro-Magnons lived in Europe, the Middle East, and North Africa. Around 30,000 years ago they began to develop better tools. They also made needles to sew clothing and spears and harpoons to hunt animals and fish. Language helped them coordinate their hunts.

Around this time humans began to create art. Stone carvings by native Australians are among the most ancient. Later prehistoric art includes paintings of animals such as deer, horses, and bison on the walls of caves in Europe, as well as sculptures in bone, stone, and clay.

NEANDERTHAL RELATIONS

Neanderthals lived in Europe and Mediterranean lands until around 30,000 years ago. Short, powerful, and stocky, they were adapted for survival in cold climates. Fossils from Israel show how Neanderthals and modern humans moved in and out of the area as the climate changed over thousands of years.

Evidence from Africa shows that Neanderthals were probably not the ancestors of modern people from these areas. A remarkable fossil of a child found in 1998 in Portugal had a blend of Neanderthal and human characteristics. This suggests that on occasions humans and Neanderthals did interbreed.

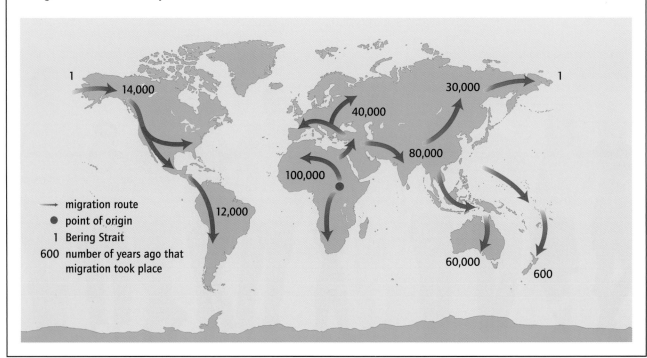

14,000

30,000

40,000

80,000

100,000

12,000

→ migration route
● point of origin
1 Bering Strait
600 number of years ago that migration took place

60,000

600

OUT OF AFRICA—THE PROOF

Homo sapiens evolved from other hominids around 250,000 years ago. A great deal of controversy has surrounded the question of where this took place. Some biologists thought that modern humans migrated from Africa recently, swiftly supplanting other humanlike hominids around the world. This is called the "Out of Africa" scenario. A separate school of thought—called **multiregionalism**—held that modern humans evolved many times in different places in Asia, Europe, and Africa from hominids that left Africa much earlier.

Dramatic fossil finds in 2003, however, have conclusively proven that the "Out of Africa" scenario is correct. The fossils, from Herto, Ethiopia, date from around 250,000 years ago and include the skulls of three individuals. They exhibit a blend of modern features and those found in ancestral species such as *Homo heidelbergensis*. The fossils support genetic evidence suggesting the time and place of the appearance of modern humans. Modern humans evolved in Africa and spread from there across the world.

Around 11,000 years ago people in the Middle East begin to raise crops and keep domestic animals. Abandoning hunting, these people became farmers, and the first towns developed. More advances swiftly followed, including the development of writing. Civilization as we know it had begun.

SCIENCE WORDS

- **Australopithecines** An early hominid group that lived in Southern Africa between 4.5 and 1 million years ago.
- **hominid** Member of the family Hominidae, to which people belong.
- **multiregionalism** Theory that modern humans evolved many times in different places in Asia, Europe, and Africa from hominids that left Africa much earlier.
- **Neanderthal** An early hominid that lived in Europe, Asia, and the Mediterranean as early as 350,000 years ago.

This artwork compares the skull shape of a Neanderthal with that of a modern human of European descent.

NEANDERTHAL

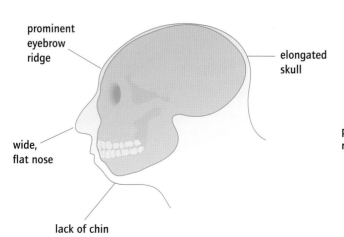

prominent eyebrow ridge

elongated skull

wide, flat nose

lack of chin

MODERN PERSON OF EUROPEAN DESCENT

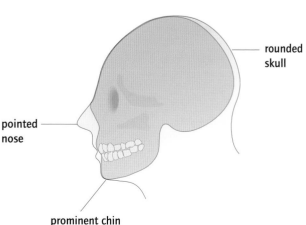

rounded skull

pointed nose

prominent chin

GLOSSARY

allele Any of the alternative forms of a gene that may occur at a given point on a chromosome.

allopatric speciation The formation of new species through geographic isolation.

anatomy Structural makeup of an organism.

antibiotic Drug that kills bacteria.

asexual reproduction Production of young without the need for mating or the fusion of sex cells.

Australopithecines An early hominid group that lived in Southern Africa between 4.5 and 1 million years ago.

biogeography The study of where organisms live and how they got there.

biological arms race The coevolution of predators and their prey.

chromosome Structure in the nucleus that contains DNA.

classification The organization of different organisms into related groups by biologists.

coevolution Evolution involving changes in two species that depend on each other to survive.

convergent evolution When distantly related creatures evolve similar body plans in response to similar environments.

creationism Theory that organisms were created by God and do not evolve.

cryptic species Species that is indistinguishable from another without genetic study.

deoxyribonucleic acid (DNA) Molecule that contains the genetic code for all cellular (nonvirus) organisms.

enzyme Protein that speeds up chemical reactions inside an organism.

eukaryote Cell containing organelles; animals, plants, and fungi are eukaryotes.

evolution Process of change in groups of organisms over long periods of time.

extinct When the last individual of a species dies.

fertilization The fusion of a sperm with an egg.

fitness The relative ability of an organism to survive and produce viable young.

fossil The remains or traces of long-dead organisms replaced by minerals.

founder effect Phenomenon that causes low genetic diversity and unusual genes to be expressed in populations (such as those on islands) founded by just a few individuals.

gene Section of DNA that codes for the structure of a protein.

gene flow Passage of genes through a geographically linked population.

gene pool The total variation of genes in a population.

genetic bottleneck Loss of genetic diversity caused by very low population levels.

genetic drift The random loss of genetic diversity; especially important in small populations or ones on islands.

geologist Scientist who studies rocks.

hominid Member of the family Hominidae, to which people belong.

hormone Chemical messenger that regulates life processes inside an organism.

hybrid Young produced by breeding between individuals of different species.

inbreeding depression Lack of fitness due to inbreeding, caused by a buildup of recessive genes.

iterative evolution Repeated evolution of similar structures in different groups over long periods of time.

Lamarckism Outdated evolutionary theory that suggested that a parent's features changed according to use during its lifetime before being inherited by young.

lipid One of a group of molecules that form oils, fats, and waxes.

mass extinction A relatively swift die-off of large numbers of species.

meiosis Cell division that leads to the production of sex cells.

minimum viable population The smallest possible population a species can tolerate before extinction becomes inevitable.

multiregionalism Theory that modern humans evolved many times in different places in Asia, Europe, and Africa from hominids that left Africa much earlier.

mutation A change to a gene; can be neutral (have no effect), negative, or positive.

natural selection Theory that only the fittest organisms survive and reproduce; one of the causes of evolution.

Neanderthal An early hominid that lived throughout Europe, Asia, and the Mediterranean as early as 350,000 years ago.

neo-Darwinism Branch of evolutionary theory that incorporates natural selection with advances in the understanding of genetics.

niche The ecological role of an organism in an ecosystem.

paleontologist Scientist who studies fossils.

polymer A long chain of molecules.

polyploid Organism with extra sets of chromosomes.

predator Animal that catches other animals for food.

prokaryote Single-celled organism, such as a bacterium, that does not contain miniorgans.

protein Molecule formed by amino acids.

punctuated equilibrium Theory that rapid bursts of evolutionary change are separated by much longer periods of little change.

recombination The shuffling of genes during sexual reproduction. It leads to increased genetic diversity.

reproductive isolation The separation of one population from another so they cannot interbreed.

ribonucleic acid (RNA) Chemical similar to DNA involved in protein production.

sexual dimorphism Anatomical differences between males and females of the same species.

sexual reproduction Production of young through the fusion of sex cells, often after mating between a male and a female.

sexual selection Form of natural selection driven by an organism's preference for characteristics in a mate.

species A group of organisms that can potentially mate with each other to produce young that can also interbreed successfully.

spontaneous generation Ancient belief that organisms could arise directly from nonliving matter.

subspecies Subdivision of a species; a population that may have different colorings and a different range than other subspecies but can still interbreed with them.

sympatric speciation The formation of new species through behavioral and other mechanisms rather than geographic isolation.

vertebrate Animal with a backbone.

vestigial structure An organ or structure that has become redundant, or may be used for a completely different purpose from its original function.

zygote An egg fertilized by a sperm that will develop into a new organism.

FURTHER RESOURCES

PUBLICATIONS

Ackroyd, P. *The Beginning*. London, UK: Dorling Kindersley, 2003.

Dawkins, R. *The Blind Watchmaker: Why the Evidence of Evolution Reveals a Universe without Design*. New York: W. W. Norton, 1996.

Day, T. *Routes of Science: Genetics*. San Diego, CA: Blackbirch Press, 2004.

Futuyma, D. *Evolution*. Sunderland, MA: Sinauer Associates Inc., 2009.

Gates, P. *Horrible Science: Evolve or Die*. New York: Scholastic, 1999.

Gould, S. J. *Wonderful Life: The Burgess Shale and the Nature of History*. New York: W. W. Norton, 1989.

Howard, J. *Darwin: A Very Short Introduction*. New York: Oxford University Press, 2001.

Loxton, D. *Evolution: How We and All Living Things Came to Be*. Toronto, CA: Kids Can Press, 2010.

Mayr, E. *What Evolution Is*. New York: BasicBooks, 2001.

Olson, S. *Mapping Human History: Discovering the Past through Our Genes*. Boston, MA: Houghton Mifflin Co., 2002.

Ward, D. and Walker, C. *DK Handbook: Fossils*. New York: DK Publishing, 2000.

WEB SITES

American Museum of Natural History: Timelines
www.amnh.org/exhibitions/Fossil_Halls/Timelines/index.html
Learn about animals and the places in which they lived from millions of years ago to 19,000 years ago.

Charles Darwin Foundation
darwinfoundation.org
Website dedicated to the conservation of the Galápagos Islands and to the work of Darwin.

The Dinosaur with a Heart
www.dinoheart.org
Pictures, animated scans, and text explain why paleontologists think dinosaurs were warm-blooded animals.

Evolution in Motion
biologyinmotion.com/evol/index.html
Do-it-yourself evolution! Test the effects of selection, mutation, and chance on the evolution of a particular trait.

Human Evolution
www.bbc.co.uk/science/cavemen/chronology
Take a journey through time, from the last ancestor of chimps and humans to the emergence of modern people.

Life in Extreme Environments
www.astrobiology.com/extreme.html
See how scientists study the possibility of life on other planets by studying life in harsh environments on Earth.

Mutant Frogs
www.pca.state.mn.us/hot/frogs.html
Learn about Minnesota's mutant frogs.

Our editors have reviewed the Web sites that appear here to ensure that they are suitable for children and students. However, many Web sites frequently change or are removed, and we cannot guarantee that a site's future contents will continue to meet our high standards of quality. Be advised that children should be closely supervised whenever they access the Internet.

INDEX

Page numbers in *italics* refer to illustrations.

WITHDRAWN